K

Zaner-Bloser, Inc., P.O. Box 16764, Columbus, Ohio 43216-6764

1-800-421-3018

Copyright © 2003 Zaner-Bloser, Inc.   ISBN 0-7367-1217-8

Printed in the United States of America

05 06 (106) 5

Zaner-Bloser
Handwriting
Opens the Door to Communication

Long proven to be a fundamental part of any language arts curriculum, handwriting instruction builds communication skills for a lifetime. Zaner-Bloser Handwriting uses an easy step-by-step approach to teach handwriting, so that students develop a solid foundation skill that encourages and supports all of their writing, reading, and assessment efforts.

With Zaner-Bloser Handwriting, students are prepared for a lifetime of communication success!

Handwriting Success:

The four Keys to Legibility—shape, size, spacing, and slant—are presented within an easy, step-by-step process for teaching and learning good handwriting.

Writing Success:

Zaner-Bloser's systematic program builds automaticity in reproduction of the alphabet, so students are free to focus on meaning and expression as they write.

Reading Success:

Zaner-Bloser's vertical manuscript alphabet improves letter recognition and supports reading development because it is the same alphabet children see outside the classroom, every day.

Better Assessment:

The Keys to Legibility help students self-assess and improve their own handwriting. Then they apply their good handwriting skills in all testing situations, including standardized tests.

Aa Bb Cc Dd Ee Ff Gg

"Handwriting is a basic communication skill that is used early in the school life of a student. To facilitate communication, it is imperative that students write legibly with ease and fluency."

Research-based Findings on Handwriting, Harford County Public Schools, Bel Air, MD

"The mental processes involved in handwriting, experts point out, are connected to other important learning functions, such as storing information in memory, retrieving information, manipulating letters, and linking them to sound when spelling."

Handwriting Instruction: Key to Good Writing, Cheryl Murfin Bond

"Solid familiarity with the visual shapes of the individual letters is an absolute prerequisite for learning to read."

Beginning to Read: Thinking and Learning About Print, Marilyn Jager Adams

Research confirms that good handwriting opens the door to communication.

"Beginning writers need regular and guided handwriting practice."

Handwriting: A Communication Tool, Saskatchewan Education

"Good handwriting and the ability to write strong compositions, it turns out, go hand-in-hand."

Handwriting Instruction: Key to Good Writing, Cheryl Murfin Bond

Zaner-Bloser
Handwriting
Opens the Door to Handwriting Success

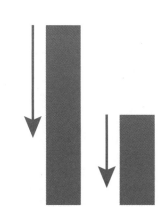

Basic Strokes **Vertical Lines**
You use vertical lines when you write.
Place your vertical strokes here.
Trace them with your finger.

Find vertical lines in the picture.
Draw this picture or one of your own.

15

Kindergarten
Student Edition
page shown.

Learning the Basic Strokes Gets Kindergartners Started

- **The Keys to Legibility are modeled rather than explicitly identified in Kindergarten.**

- **Major emphasis is placed on learning the basic strokes as a foundation for legibility.**

- **Students learn a basic stroke, then they immediately identify the shape in nature and in letters.**

- **Every Kindergarten Student Edition includes sturdy manipulatives that represent the basic strokes.**

The Program Components Students and Teachers Need for Handwriting Success

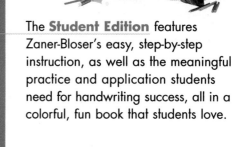

The **Student Edition** features Zaner-Bloser's easy, step-by-step instruction, as well as the meaningful practice and application students need for handwriting success, all in a colorful, fun book that students love.

The **Teacher Edition** is fully annotated and provides teachers a step-by-step guide that makes teaching handwriting simply successful.

Practice Masters provide even more practice for every letter and skill students learn, as well as additional resources to make teaching successful —certificates, an evaluation record, and school to home letters to keep parents and guardians involved.

The **Poster/Wall Chart Super Pack** is a perfect addition to the handwriting classroom, with Manuscript and Cursive Alphabet Posters, a Keys to Legibility Poster, and a Handwriting Positions Poster.

Handwriting Ancillary Materials
That Support the Instructional Plan

All of these Handwriting ancillary materials are provided FREE upon request with purchase of 25 matching Student Editions—the essentials you need to reinforce Zaner-Bloser's handwriting instruction are included!

Teacher Edition with
Grade Level Evaluation
Guide included

Practice Masters

Poster/Wall Chart
Super Pack

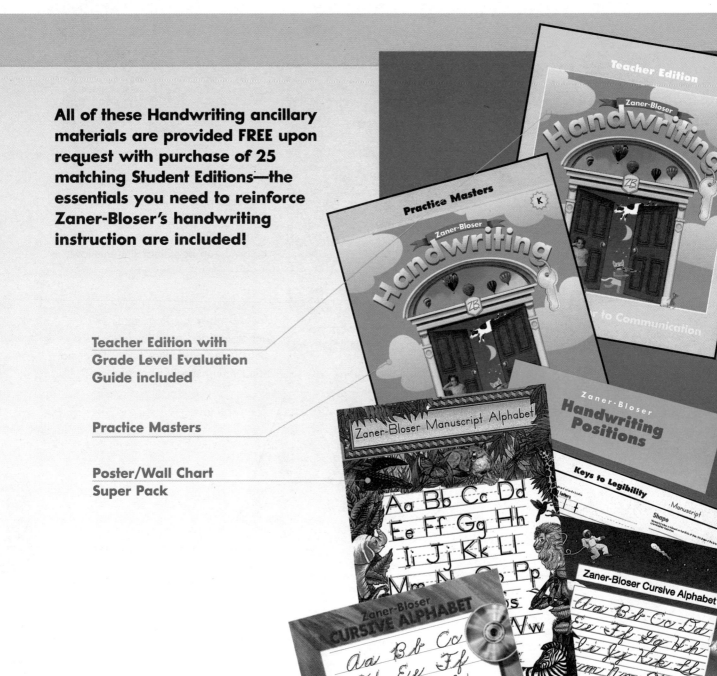

Handwriting Ancillary Materials
to Further Enhance the Handwriting Classroom

These ancillaries are referenced at the beginning of every unit in the Teacher Edition:

A Alphabet Wall Strips, K–6

B Illustrated Alphabet Strips, K–4

C Desk Strips, 1–6

D Wipe-Off Practice Cards—Manuscript and Cursive, K–6

E Zaner-Bloser Fontware, K–6

F Manuscript/Cursive Card Sets, 1–4

G Home Handwriting Pack, K–4

H Handwriting Tools, K–6

I Journals and Blank Books, K–6

J Paper, K–6

K Modality Kit

L Listening Alphabeat, 1–4

M Post Office Kit, K–4

N Escritura—Spanish Blackline Masters, 1–6

O Fun With Handwriting

P Touch & Trace Letter Cards, PreK–3

Q Now I Know My ABC's, PreK–1

R Now I Know My 123's, PreK–1

S Read, Write, and Color Alphabet Mat, K–2

T Letter Cards, K–2

U Book of Transparencies, 1–6

V Handwriting Research and Resources

W Opens the Door to Teaching Handwriting— CD-ROM for Classroom or Teacher Inservice Use

Only Zaner-Bloser provides you with this much support for teaching handwriting!

Fine Motor Development Kit

Zaner-Bloser's Fine Motor Development Kit can help your students develop the fine motor skills essential for writing and many other school activities.

The Student Edition
Opens the Door to Handwriting Success
for Students

Zaner-Bloser Handwriting guides students through an easy step-by-step process for learning good, legible handwriting that will last a lifetime.

Letter models with arrows show stroke description and sequence.

Shaded letters and words for tracing are provided.

Starting dots tell students where to begin the letter.

Stop and Check signs remind students to evaluate their letters.

School to Home stroke descriptions help parents reinforce and evaluate students' handwriting at home.

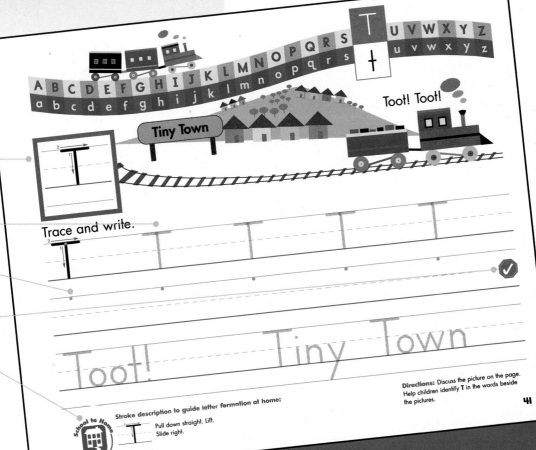

Trace and write.

Toot! Tiny Town

Directions: Discuss the picture on the page. Help children identify **T** in the words beside the pictures.

41

Stroke description to guide letter formation at home:

Pull down straight. Lift.
Slide right.

A Practice page in each section gives students another chance to practice and review the letters they just learned.

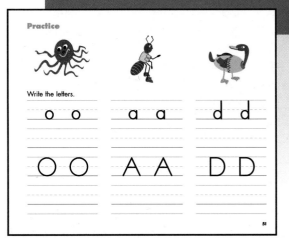

Practice

Write the letters.

o o   a a   d d

O O   A A   D D

51

Kindergarten Student Edition pages shown.

Z8

Writing practice is done directly beneath a model that gives students a visual guide that both left- and right-handed students can easily see.

Tracing words provides students with even more writing practice.

Trace and write.

train

tower

train   tower   track

Directions: Discuss the picture on the page. Help children identify t in the words that name the pictures.

Stroke description to guide letter formation at home:
Pull down straight. Lift. Slide right.

42

A Write the Alphabet page in each section showcases children's ability to write letters from memory.

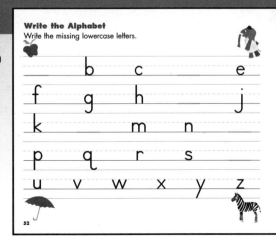

Write the Alphabet
Write the missing lowercase letters.

b   c   e

f   g   h   j

k   m   n

p   q   r   s

u   v   w   x   y   z

52

Kindergarten
Student Edition
pages shown.

The Teacher Edition
Opens the Door
to Handwriting Success
for Teachers

The Book Opener provides the information, guidance, and extra materials teachers want.

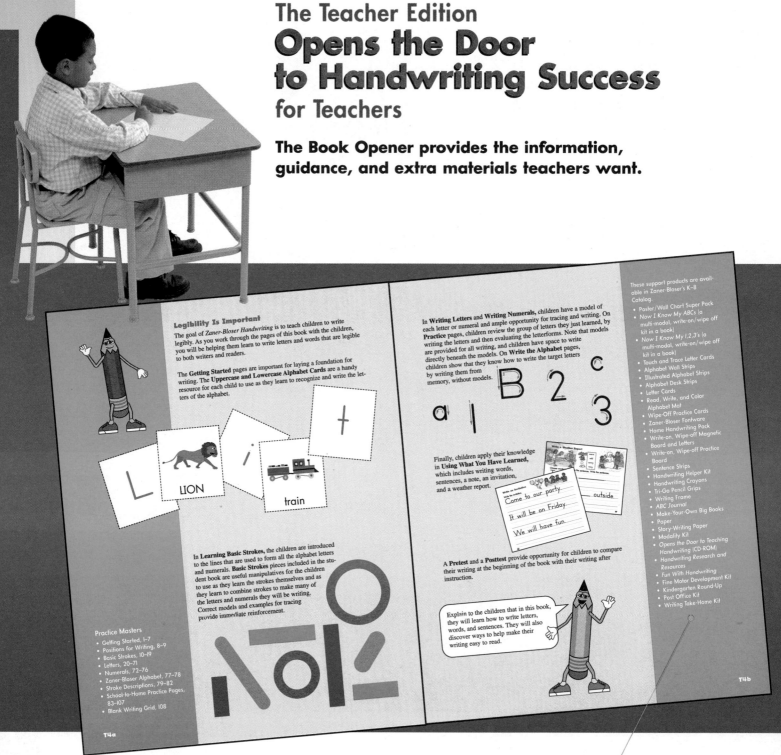

Legibility Is Important

The goal of *Zaner-Bloser Handwriting* is to teach children to write legibly. As you work through the pages of this book with the children, you will be helping them learn to write letters and words that are legible to both writers and readers.

The **Getting Started** pages are important for laying a foundation for writing. The **Uppercase and Lowercase Alphabet Cards** are a handy resource for each child to use as they learn to recognize and write the letters of the alphabet.

In **Learning Basic Strokes,** the children are introduced to the lines that are used to form all the alphabet letters and numerals. **Basic Strokes** pieces included in the student book are useful manipulatives for the children to use as they learn the strokes themselves and as they learn to combine strokes to make many of the letters and numerals they will be writing. Correct models and examples for tracing provide immediate reinforcement.

Practice Masters
- Getting Started, 1–7
- Positions for Writing, 8–9
- Basic Strokes, 10–19
- Letters, 20–71
- Numerals, 72–76
- Zaner-Bloser Alphabet, 77–78
- Stroke Descriptions, 79–82
- School-to-Home Practice Pages, 83–107
- Blank Writing Grid, 108

T4a

In **Writing Letters** and **Writing Numerals,** children have a model of each letter or numeral and ample opportunity for tracing and writing. On **Practice** pages, children review the group of letters they just learned, by writing the letters and then evaluating the letterforms. Note that models are provided for all writing, and children have space to write directly beneath the models. On **Write the Alphabet** pages, children show that they know how to write the target letters by writing them from memory, without models.

Finally, children apply their knowledge in **Using What You Have Learned,** which includes writing words, sentences, a note, an invitation, and a weather report.

Come to our party
It will be on Friday
We will have fun

A **Pretest** and a **Posttest** provide opportunity for children to compare their writing at the beginning of the book with their writing after instruction.

Explain to the children that in this book, they will learn how to write letters, words, and sentences. They will also discover ways to help make their writing easy to read.

These support products are available in Zaner-Bloser's K–8 Catalog.
- Poster/Wall Chart Super Pack
- Now I Know My ABCs (a multi-modal, write-on/wipe off kit in a book)
- Now I Know My 1,2,3's (a multi-modal, write-on/wipe off kit in a book)
- Touch and Trace Letter Cards
- Alphabet Wall Strips
- Illustrated Alphabet Strips
- Alphabet Desk Strips
- Letter Cards
- Read, Write, and Color Alphabet Mat
- Wipe-Off Practice Cards
- Zaner-Bloser Fontware
- Home Handwriting Pack
- Write-on, Wipe-off Magnetic Board and Letters
- Write-on, Wipe-off Practice Board
- Sentence Strips
- Handwriting Helper Kit
- Handwriting Crayons
- Tri-Go Pencil Grips
- Writing Frame
- ABC Journal
- Make-Your-Own Big Books
- Paper
- Story-Writing Paper
- Modality Kit
- Opens the Door to Teaching Handwriting (CD-ROM)
- Handwriting Research and Resources
- Fun With Handwriting
- Fine Motor Development Kit
- Kindergarten Round-Up
- Post Office Kit
- Writing Take-Home Kit

T4b

Kindergarten
Teacher Edition
pages shown.

Each section of the book is identified and explained to help teachers plan their handwriting curriculum.

Additional materials are listed that support the instructional plan.

Zaner-Bloser
Handwriting
Opens the Door to Successful Time Management
for Teachers

Three-step lesson takes about 15 minutes!

The three steps of the lesson present clear, simple teaching guidelines.

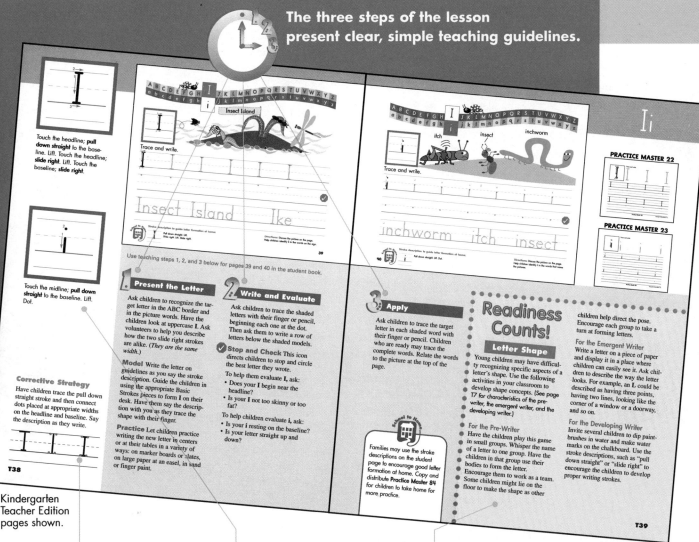

Kindergarten Teacher Edition pages shown.

Corrective strategies & coaching hints provide the means to correct common problems.

Stroke descriptions are short and clearly marked.

Developmentally appropriate activities provide tips for teaching students who are at different developmental stages of handwriting.

Zaner-Bloser Handwriting Opens the Door to Writing and Reading Success

Teaching Handwriting in the 21st Century— An Occupational Therapist's Perspective

By Maureen King, O.T.R.

Children come to school with a broad range of developmental skill levels. Many children are already using many fine motor skills, gross motor skills, and perceptual skills, developed through exposure to a variety of play experiences. Some children, however, have not properly developed these fundamental skills that directly impact how well they learn in school.

Hand (motor) skills, as they develop, build upon each other, beginning at birth when babies grasp reflexively. As children grow and interact with their surroundings, they move on to using their thumbs and index fingers, and then their hands in a variety of positions. The development of perceptual skills, a child's ability to perceive how things fit together, is best facilitated by assembling and moving objects around.

In the past, there were more "play-filled" opportunities to prompt development of these skills. Today, however, children's play is becoming more automated. Many board games are now played on computer screens, shoes are fastened with Velcro, and crayons are put aside in order to pursue interactive activities. This decreased use of manipulatives at home and at school can diminish a child's opportunity to practice grasp and release and controlled placement—skills that are necessary for efficient pencil use.

Symptoms of these trends can manifest themselves in a young child's first handwriting experiences at school. Handwriting requires eye-hand coordination, fine motor skills, and the perceptual ability to simultaneously understand and produce letterforms. When children who have not developed key foundational skills first attempt to write manuscript letters, frustration can result. Often, their efforts consist of incomplete or careless methods of forming letters, which can lead to bad habits. Something must be done for these children so that they can achieve handwriting success.

I am pleased to offer structured corrective strategies that will help teachers strengthen skills that lead to improved handwriting. You will find these strategies, or **Special Helps,** throughout the **Zaner-Bloser Handwriting** Teacher Edition. They suggest ways to isolate component skills, reinforce the instructional material, and highlight special points and concerns. In using these ideas in your classroom, include a mix of learning styles so that children can see it, hear it, feel it, do it in their palms and on the chalkboard, with their eyes open and closed. These activities will help bring handwriting success to all children, including those who rarely play board games, color with crayons, or tie their shoes.

Maureen King is referenced throughout the K–3 Teacher Editions.

The Critical Role of Handwriting in Student Success

By Steve Graham, Professor and Distinguished Scholar/Teacher, University of Maryland

Handwriting plays a critical role in writing development. One way of illustrating its impact on writing is to imagine that you have been asked to write something using a Chinese typewriter. This is the most complicated typewriter in the world, containing 5,850 characters. As you search for characters, some of the ideas and writing plans you are trying to hold in memory will undoubtedly be lost, as most of your attention is consumed by trying to transcribe words into print. It will also be difficult to create additional plans or sharpen the text you are currently producing, as most of your attention is directed at locating the next character to be typed.

Although most of us will never use a Chinese typewriter, we have at one time or another experienced frustration at being unable to write our thoughts down fast enough due to our limited handwriting ability. For children, handwriting can be so "taxing" that it influences the pace and course of their writing development. The physical act of handwriting is so strenuous for many beginning writers that they develop an approach to writing that minimizes the use of other composing processes, such as planning, because these processes are also mentally demanding. Just as importantly, children who experience difficulty mastering handwriting often avoid writing and develop a mind-set that they cannot write, leading to arrested writing development.

Poor handwriting is also the thief of one of our most valuable commodities—time. Teachers lose precious time trying to decipher papers that are illegible. The handwriting of some children is so slow that it takes them almost twice as long to produce the same text as their more facile classmates, exerting a heavy toll on their productivity.

Despite the importance of handwriting to school success, writing development, and written communication, the teaching of handwriting has been de-emphasized in some schools. Although handwriting continues to be taught in most classrooms nationwide, it is taught sporadically, if at all, in others. In these classrooms, it is often assumed that handwriting will develop naturally, by immersing children in a literacy-rich environment where they have plenty of opportunities to write and read for real purposes. While this assumption has a comforting simplicity, absolving schools from the responsibility of directly teaching handwriting, there is no scientific evidence to support it. In contrast, there is almost a century of research that demonstrates the power of directly and systematically teaching handwriting.

For years, I have heard rumors about the demise of handwriting, as it would soon be replaced by word processing or speech synthesis (prior to that it was the typewriter). While these tools have clearly become a more prominent part of everyday life, handwriting has not been superseded. Much writing is still done by hand, especially in schools, and this is unlikely to change anytime in the near future.

Steve Graham is referenced in the Teacher Editions.

Promote Writing and Reading Development

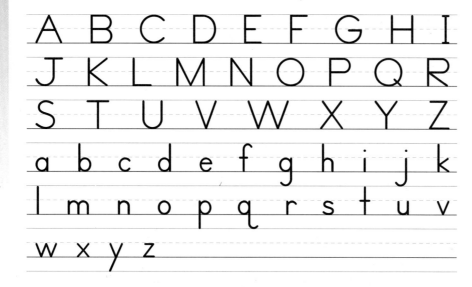

Zaner-Bloser's continuous-stroke, vertical manuscript alphabet . . .

- Promotes automaticity in students' writing because students only have to learn four simple strokes

- Reinforces students' reading because it is the alphabet students see every day inside and outside the classroom

Two Simplified Alphabets for Handwriting and Communication Success

Zaner-Bloser's simplified cursive alphabet . . .

- Reinforces writing and reading development because it is easier to write and read

- Helps students get higher test scores because, as legible cursive writing becomes automatic, students can focus more energy on their message

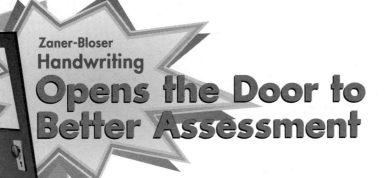

Zaner-Bloser
Handwriting
Opens the Door to Better Assessment

Write an Invitation

Write the invitation.

Come to our party.

It will be on Friday.

We will have fun.

116

Write a Weather Report

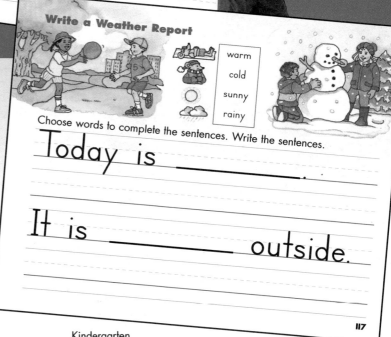

warm
cold
sunny
rainy

Choose words to complete the sentences. Write the sentences.

Today is _____.

It is _____ outside.

117

Kindergarten
Student Edition
pages shown.

Better Self-Assessment:

Stop and Check signs throughout the lessons are reminders for students to continuously self-evaluate as they work.

More Success on Standardized Tests:

Kindergartners begin by practicing real-life handwriting situations. This helps them develop automaticity in writing and do well in testing situations later on, where legibility is important to success.

Zaner-Bloser Handwriting

Opens the Door to Handwriting Success for Every Student

Handwriting success is achieved most often when the initial instruction involves a multimodal approach. Students need to develop a correct mental and motor image of the stroke, joining, letter, or word before they attempt to write.

Throughout the Teacher Edition, Zaner-Bloser Handwriting provides techniques that will help address the multimodal needs of different students.

For the Kinesthetic Learner—Remember that instruction for the student whose primary sensory modality is kinesthetic should be tactile, involving movement and the sense of touch.

- Walk out the letter strokes on the floor.
- Form letters in the air using full-arm movement.
- Make letter models with clay or string.
- Write strokes, letters, and joinings in sand.
- Use different writing instruments, such as crayons, markers, and varied sizes of pencils.
- Trace large strokes, letters, and joinings on the chalkboard and on paper—first with fingers, then with chalk or other media.
- Dip fingers in water and form letters and joinings on the chalkboard.

For the Auditory Learner—Students whose primary sensory modality is auditory require instruction that enables them to listen and to verbalize.

- Verbalize each stroke in the letter as that letter is presented.
- Encourage the student to verbalize the letter strokes and to explain how strokes are alike and how they are different in the letterforms.
- Ask students to write random letters as you verbalize the strokes.
- Be consistent in the language you use to describe letters, strokes, shapes, and joinings.

For the Visual Learner—As a general rule, a student whose primary sensory modality is visual will have little difficulty in handwriting if instruction includes adequate visual stimuli.

- Encourage students first to look at the letter as a whole and to ask themselves if the letter is tall or short, fat or skinny. Does all of the letter rest on the baseline, is it a tall letter, or is it a letter with a descender? How many and what kinds of strokes are in the letter?
- Have students look at each individual stroke carefully before they attempt to write the letter.

The Left-Handed Student

Three important techniques assist the left-handed
student in writing.

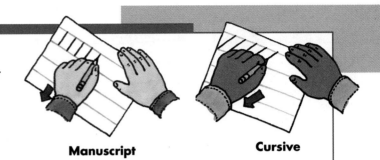

Paper Position:

For manuscript writing, the lower right corner of the paper
should point toward the left of the body's midsection.

For cursive writing, the lower right corner of the paper
should point toward the body's midsection.

Downstrokes are pulled toward the left elbow.

Manuscript   **Cursive**

Pencil Position:

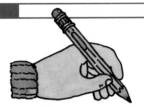

The top of the pencil should point toward the left elbow. The pen or pencil
should be held at least one inch above the point. This allows students to
see what they are writing.

Arm Position:

Holding the left arm close to the body and keeping the hand below the
line of writing prevents "hooking" the wrist and smearing the writing.

General Coaching Tips for Teachers

- Teach a handwriting lesson daily, if possible, for
  approximately 15 minutes. Spend a minimum of
  5 minutes of this time in actual instruction before
  the students practice.

- Surround children with models of good handwriting.
  Set an example when you write on the chalkboard
  and on students' papers.

- Teach the letters through basic strokes.

- Emphasize one **Key to Legibility** at a time.

- Use appropriately ruled paper. Increase the size of
  the grids for any student who is experiencing difficulty.

- Continuous self-evaluation is necessary for
  optimal progress.

- Stress comfortable writing posture and pencil
  position. Increase the size of the pencil for
  students who "squeeze" the writing implement.

- Show the alternate method of holding the pencil,
  and allow students to choose the one that is better
  for them. (Refer to the alternate method shown in
  the Teacher Edition.)

- Provide opportunities for children in the upper
  grades to use manuscript writing. Permit manuscript
  for some assignments if children prefer manuscript
  to cursive.

- Encourage students with poor sustained motor control
  to use conventional manuscript, with frequent lifts,
  if continuous manuscript is difficult for them.

Meeting Individual Needs

Students With Reversal Tendencies

Directionality—A problem with directionality (moving from left to right across the page) interferes with a child's ability to form letters correctly and to write text that makes sense. To develop correct directionality, try these techniques:

- Provide opportunities for the child to write at the chalkboard within a confined area with frequent arrows as a reminder of left-to-right progression.

- Prepare sheets of paper on which the left edges and the beginning stroke of a letter, such as **b**, are colored green.

Letter Reversals—Determine which letters a student most often reverses. Make a list of these reversals and concentrate on them either on an individual basis or by grouping together the students who are reversing the same letters.

- Emphasize each step of the stroke description before the children write a letter.

- Provide a letter for tracing that has been colored according to stroke order. Repeat the stroke description with the children as they write the letter.

- Encourage the children to write the letter as they verbalize the stroke description.

Students With Attention Deficit Problems

Because they have difficulty focusing and maintaining attention, these students must concentrate on individual strokes in the letterforms. When they have learned the strokes, they can put them together to form letters, and then learn the joinings (in cursive) to write words. The activities recommended for kinesthetic learners (on page Z16) are appropriate for students with an attention deficit problem. Following are additional suggestions:

- Give very short assignments.

- Supervise closely and give frequent encouragement.

Zaner-Bloser
Handwriting
K

Author
Clinton S. Hackney, Ed.D.

Reviewers
Julie Althide, Teacher, Hazelwood School District, St. Louis, Missouri
Becky Brashears, Teacher, Gocio Elementary, Sarasota, Florida
Douglas Dewey, Teacher, National Heritage Academies, Grand Rapids, Michigan
Jennifer B. Dutcher, Teacher, Elk Grove School District, Sacramento, California
Gita Farbman, Teacher, School District of Philadelphia, Philadelphia, Pennsylvania
Susan Ford, Teacher, St. Ann's School, Charlotte, North Carolina
Brenda Forehand, Teacher, David Lipscomb Middle School, Nashville, Tennessee
Sharon Hall, Teacher, USD 443, Dodge City, Kansas
Sr. James Madeline, Teacher, St. Anthony School, Allston, Massachusetts

Lori A. Martin, Teacher, Chicago Public Schools, Chicago, Illinois
Vikki F. McCurdy, Teacher, Mustang School District, Oklahoma City, Oklahoma
Melissa Neary Morgan, Reading Specialist, Fairfax County Public Schools, Fairfax, Virginia
Sue Postlewait, Literacy Resource Consultant, Marshall County Schools, Moundsville, West Virginia
Gloria C. Rivera, Principal, Edinburg CISO, Edinburg, Texas
Rebecca Rollefson, Teacher, Ericsson Community School, Minneapolis, Minnesota
Susan Samsa, Teacher, Dover City Schools, Dover, Ohio
Zelda J. Smith, Instructional Specialist, New Orleans Public Schools, New Orleans, Louisiana

Early Childhood Consultant: Jo Beecher Prather, Reading and Early Childhood Specialist, Madison County School District, Madison, MS
Occupational Therapy Consultant: Maureen E. King, O.T.R.

Credits
Art: Mariano Gil: 3, 4, 6, 8, 9, 37, 38, 39, 40, 41, 42, 43, 45, 46, 47, 48, 49, 50, 51, 53, 54, 55, 56, 57, 58, 59, 61, 62, 63, 64, 65, 66, 67, 69, 70, 71, 72, 73, 74, 75, 76, 77, 79, 80, 81, 82, 83, 84, 85, 86, 87, 89, 90, 91, 92, 93, 94, 95, 97, 98, 99, 100, 101, 102, 103, 118, 119; Susan Lexa: 4, 112, 113, 114, 115, 116, 117; Sharron O'Neil: 3, 16, 17, 20, 21, 24, 25, 28, 29, 32, 33, 35, 36, 105, 106, 107, 108, 109, 110, 111; Andy San Diego: 10, 11

Photos: George C. Anderson Photography, Inc.: 12–13

Development: Kirchoff/Wohlberg, Inc., in collaboration with Zaner-Bloser Educational Publishers

ISBN 0-7367-1209-7   02 03 04 05 06 159 5 4 3 2 1

Copyright © 2003 Zaner-Bloser, Inc.

 # Contents

Getting Started

Learning Basic Strokes

Writing Letters

Writing Numerals

Using What You Have Learned

Teacher Edition Contents

Legibility Is Important

The goal of *Zaner-Bloser Handwriting* is to teach children to write legibly. As you work through the pages of this book with the children, you will be helping them learn to write letters and words that are legible to both writers and readers.

The **Getting Started** pages are important for laying a foundation for writing. The **Uppercase and Lowercase Alphabet Cards** are a handy resource for each child to use as they learn to recognize and write the letters of the alphabet.

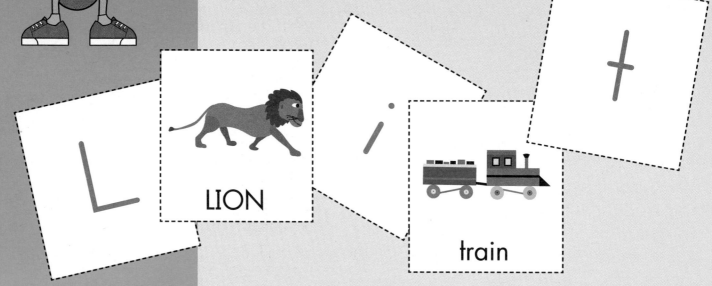

In **Learning Basic Strokes,** the children are introduced to the lines that are used to form all the alphabet letters and numerals. **Basic Strokes** pieces included in the student book are useful manipulatives for the children to use as they learn the strokes themselves and as they learn to combine strokes to make many of the letters and numerals they will be writing. Correct models and examples for tracing provide immediate reinforcement.

Practice Masters

In **Writing Letters** and **Writing Numerals,** children have a model of each letter or numeral and ample opportunity for tracing and writing. On **Practice** pages, children review the group of letters they just learned, by writing the letters and then evaluating the letterforms. Note that models are provided for all writing, and children have space to write directly beneath the models. On **Write the Alphabet** pages, children show that they know how to write the target letters by writing them from memory, without models.

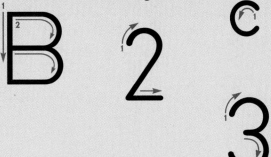

Finally, children apply their knowledge in **Using What You Have Learned,** which includes writing words, sentences, a note, an invitation, and a weather report.

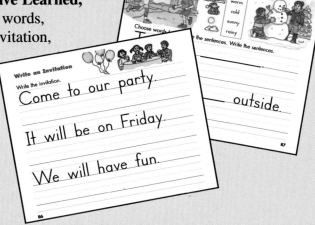

A **Pretest** and a **Posttest** provide opportunity for children to compare their writing at the beginning of the book with their writing after instruction.

Explain to the children that in this book, they will learn how to write letters, words, and sentences. They will also discover ways to help make their writing easy to read.

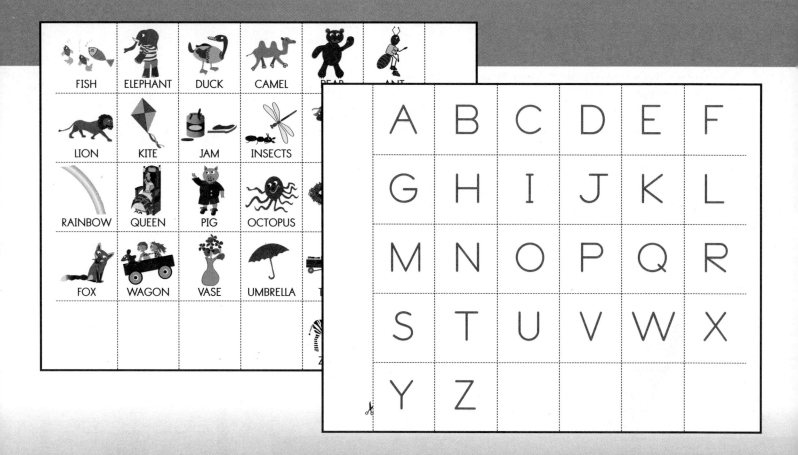

Alphabet Cards

Before they begin formal hand-writing instruction, children should be able to name and recognize most uppercase and lowercase letters of the alphabet. Readiness for handwriting is signaled by children's interest in letters and awareness of their different shapes and features.

As handwriting lessons begin, it is important to continue naming letters and discussing their appearance. Studying the shapes of letters during handwriting instruction can lead to improved letter recognition.

Use the alphabet cards on student pages 5–8 for activities that help you assess children's ability to recognize and name letters. Remove these pages from each child's book, and ask children to cut carefully on the lines to separate the letter cards. You may wish to store each child's letter cards in a zip-top plastic bag.

Provide time for children to engage in a variety of games and activities that promote letter recognition. Choose from the ideas on these two pages.

Practice Masters 1 *and* **2** *are available for use with naming the uppercase letters.*

Naming Uppercase Letters

- Ask children to select the upper-case letter cards that match letters in their first names. Then ask, "Which children have an **A** in their names?" Have those children hold up their **A** cards. Continue with other letters of the alphabet.

- Direct one partner to select several letter cards, such as **A, B, C, D,** and arrange them in a series so that the other partner can examine the letters. Have the other partner find his or her matching letter cards and place them beneath.

- Give clues to one of the letter card pictures. For example, say, "This thing seems to change its shape. It is not on our planet. It shines at night." (*MOON*) After children guess the picture, have them name the letters in the word and spell the word with their letter cards.

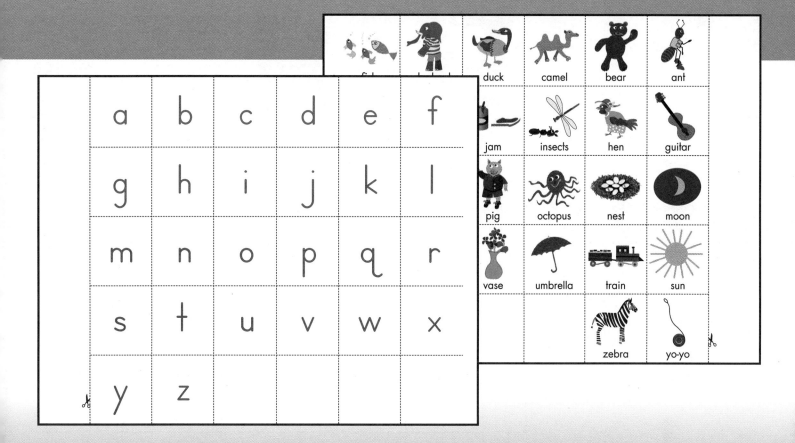

a	b	c	d	e	f
g	h	i	j	k	l
m	n	o	p	q	r
s	t	u	v	w	x
y	z				

duck · camel · bear · ant
jam · insects · hen · guitar
pig · octopus · nest · moon
vase · umbrella · train · sun
zebra · yo-yo

Naming Lowercase Letters

- Collect all the letter cards for a specific letter (e.g., all the **b** cards). Give the cards to several children and ask them to hide the cards around the classroom. Then write the target letter on the chalkboard or on chart paper. Begin the game with a chant:

  We're going on a letter hunt.
  *We're going to find some **b**'s*
  (or another letter).
  Are you ready?
  Let's go!

Invite children to walk around the room and collect the hidden letter cards.

Practice Masters 3 *and* **4** *are available for use with naming the lowercase letters.*

- Have children spread out their letter cards on their desktops, picture sides up. Then write a lowercase letter on the chalkboard or on chart paper. Ask children to look for the letter in the words that name the pictures. Write the words under the target letter. Invite a volunteer to come up and circle the target letter in each word.

- Have each child in the group choose any lowercase letter card at random and hold it up in the air. Then ask a volunteer to find children holding a specific letter that you name and to tap gently on the head the children who are holding up that letter. For example, say, "Tap all the children holding **k**." The volunteer can then name a word that begins with that letter. Continue until all children have had a turn to find letters.

Matching Uppercase and Lowercase Letters

- Distribute lowercase letter cards to half the class and the corresponding uppercase cards to the other half. On your signal, challenge the children to find their partners.

- Ask one partner to give clues to one of the pictures. After the other partner guesses the picture, have partners work together to look at the word shown in uppercase letters and find the matching lowercase letter cards, or vice versa.

Practice Masters 5, 6, *and* **7** *are available for use with matching uppercase and lowercase letters.*

Show What You Can Do

🎵 Begin With a Song 🎵

Write "The Alphabet Song" on chart paper. As you point to the letters, invite children to sing this familiar song with you.

A-B-C-D-E-F-G
H-I-J-K
L-M-N-O-P
Q-R-S
T-U-V
W-X-Y and Z.
Now I know my ABC's.
Next time won't you sing with me?

Pretest

Show What You Can Do

Draw a picture.

Write letters you know.

9

Coaching Hints

Large Writing Children whose writing is large should be given many opportunities to write at the chalkboard, on the classified ad section of the newspaper, or on newsprint with wide rules. A writing crayon is good for large writing. (kinesthetic)

Desktop Nametags Use tagboard or self-adhesive ruled name strips to make a desktop nametag for each child in your class. Tape the nametags to the children's desks so they can use them as writing models. (visual)

Present the Activity

Tell children that during handwriting time they will be learning to write the letters of the alphabet and the numerals.

Preview the book with the children. Explain that the first thing they will do is show what they can already write.

Help children locate the space where they will draw a picture and the space where they will write letters they know. If necessary, discuss possible ideas for drawing on student page 9.

Evaluate

Observe how children draw and how they write the letters. Note that some children may be writing all uppercase letters because these are the ones they sometimes learn in preparation for starting school.

Some children may have been taught to write some or all of the alphabet letters and numerals in preschool. You may use this page as a pretest to help you assess each child's present handwriting skills. Use the information on page T7 to help you determine the developmental stages of the writers in your classroom.

Note: You might want to store the pretests in a folder so children can have them later in the year to compare with the writing on their posttest.

Stages of Handwriting Development

Characteristics of the Pre-Writer

- Writing may take the form of scribbles, strings of letter-like shapes, and "pretend" writing. Often there is little distinction between drawing and writing.

- Children at this stage may know how to write their names fairly well. However, they do not demonstrate a consistent understanding of left-to-right progression and the need for spacing between letters and words.

- Pencil position often has not yet developed into the traditional tripod grip.

- It is important for adults to recognize and value early writing efforts so children learn that writing has an important purpose.

- Emphasize recognition of letters and basic strokes. Familiarity with the unique shape of each letter will greatly simplify the handwriting task.

- When children are able to name the basic strokes and write them smoothly, formal handwriting instruction can begin.

Characteristics of the Emergent Writer

- Writing may consist of alphabet letters (usually uppercase letters) and letter-like shapes. These may be placed randomly or may appear in word-like strings.

- Emergent writers attend to letter similarities and differences. They are motivated to reproduce text they see on signs and in books.

- Although children at this stage demonstrate an awareness of left-to-right progression, they often reverse letters or write upside-down.

- Children may write letters of widely varying size and leave large amounts of space in their writing, or no space at all.

- Emergent writers are gaining more control of their hands and can be easily taught to use the traditional tripod pencil grip.

- Emergent writers often develop their own methods for writing letters they see. Bad habits and inefficient letter formations can result. Handwriting instruction should focus on the correct starting point and stroke sequence for each letter.

Characteristics of the Developing Writer

- Children are beginning to write letters and familiar words with more confidence. Writing may include simple "I Love You" notes, greeting cards, signs, and labels.

- Placement of letters and words on the page demonstrates growing consistency in size and spacing, but writing may still have a "messy" overall appearance.

- Letter reversals, especially for letters that reverse direction, such as **S** and **J,** and those that are easily confused, such as **b** and **d,** are common.

- An awkward pencil grip may be a bad habit for some children at this stage. Take the time to teach and reinforce the standard tripod pencil grip.

- Handwriting instruction should include multi-sensory practice activities that will help children begin to write letters smoothly and automatically.

Left Hand/Right Hand

Before Writing

Invite the children to stand in a circle and sing and play "Looby-Loo."

Here we dance Looby-loo,
Here we dance Looby-light.
Here we dance Looby-loo,
All on a Saturday night.

I put my right hand *in,*
I put my right hand *out.*
I give my right hand *a*
*   shake, shake, shake,*
And turn myself about.

Repeat using the words *left hand,*
right foot, left foot, head, and
whole self.

You use your hands when you write.
Draw your **left** hand on this mitten.

Many children use their left hand to write.

10

Present the Activity

Direct the children to look at the mitten on student page 10. Explain that this is a mitten for the left hand. Read the text in the speech bubble with the children, and ask if any of them usually use their left hand to draw or write. Then read the directions on the page with the children and ask them to use a pencil, crayon, or marker to draw their left hand on the mitten.

Repeat the procedure for the right-hand mitten on student page 11.

Note: Children may need a partner to draw around the hand they normally would use for drawing or writing.

Show children how the index finger and extended thumb of the left hand make an **L** on their left hands. Point out the **L** near the page number on many of the left-hand pages of their books.

Coaching Hint

Left-Handedness Right-handed teachers will better understand left-handed children if they practice the left-handed position themselves. Group left-handers together for instruction if you can do so without calling attention to the practice. They should be seated to the left of the chalkboard.

Draw your **right** hand on this mitten.

Which hand do you use to hold your pencil?

Simon Says To play this variation of "Simon Says," give children directions that include the words *left* and *right*. Have them stand facing you. Remind them to follow the direction only when they hear "Simon says." Here are some ideas to get you started:

> Simon says, "Touch your nose with your right hand."
> "Touch your chin with your left hand."
> Simon says, "Take two steps to the left."

(auditory, kinesthetic)

Assessing Hand Preference

If the child is definitely left-handed, it is better to teach her or him to use that hand in writing. If, however, there is some doubt about which is the dominant hand, there are many simple play situations that the observant teacher will find helpful in determining hand dominance. A few guidelines should be observed in these procedures. Do not tell the child that she or he is being tested. Work with only one child at a time. Keep a record as to which hand is used for each specific situation. Let the child pick up the testing materials; do not hand them to the child. Keep a tally of the procedures. If the child indicates true ambidexterity, it is probably better to train the right hand. Sample test procedures are listed here.

Hand Puppet Place a hand puppet with a sleeve on the table. Observe the child in a play situation to see on which hand she or he puts the puppet.

Cutting with Scissors Place a pair of scissors and a piece of construction paper on the table. Instruct the child to cut the paper into strips. Observe which hand is used to pick up the scissors and cut the paper. Then place paper of a different color on the table and have the child repeat the process. Did the child use the same hand or change hands? Repeat with a third color.

Throwing a Ball Place a rubber ball on the floor. Ask the child to pick up the ball and toss it to you.

Holding a Spoon At lunchtime or in a play situation in which the child uses eating utensils, observe which hand is used.

Hammering Nails Place a toy hammer and nails or a peg and pegboard on the table. Observe the child as she or he hammers several nails or pegs into place.

Coaching Hint

Holding the Pencil The *Zaner-Bloser Writing Frame* can be used to show good hand position, for both left- and right-handed writers, because the hand automatically settles into the correct position. (kinesthetic)

Writing Positions

If you write with your  left hand. . .

Sit up tall.
Keep your feet on the floor.

Slant your paper.

Put both arms on the desk.

Pull your pencil toward your left elbow.

Use your right hand to move the paper.

Hold the pencil like this.

Do not squeeze the pencil when you write.

12

Use pages T10 and T11 with student pages 12 and 13.

Sitting Position

Using correct body position when writing will help children write better letters. They will also not tire as quickly. Encourage them to sit comfortably erect with their feet flat on the floor and their hips touching the back of the chair. Both arms should rest on the tabletop.

Use **Practice Masters 8** *and* **9** *for more information.*

Paper Position

Correct paper placement is vital to legibility. To assure that the paper is placed correctly, for both right- and left-handed children, use tape to form a frame on the desk so the children will be able to place the paper in the correct position.

Right-Handed Writer

Left-Handed Writer

Pencil Position

Model good pencil position for the children. The writing implement is held between the thumb and the first two fingers, about an inch above its point. The first finger rests on top of the implement. The end of the bent thumb is placed against the writing instrument to hold it high in the hand and near the knuckle.

Left Hand

Right Hand

If you write with your  right hand...

Sit up tall.
Keep both feet on the floor.

Keep your paper straight.

Put both arms on the desk.

Pull your pencil toward the middle of your body.

Use your left hand to move the paper.

Hold the pencil like this.

Do not squeeze the pencil when you write.

13

Coaching Hint

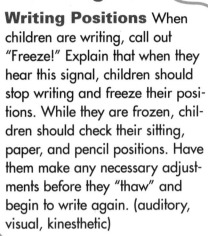

Writing Positions When children are writing, call out "Freeze!" Explain that when they hear this signal, children should stop writing and freeze their positions. While they are frozen, children should check their sitting, paper, and pencil positions. Have them make any necessary adjustments before they "thaw" and begin to write again. (auditory, visual, kinesthetic)

Note: Children who have difficulty with the traditional pencil position may prefer the alternate method of holding the pencil between the first and second fingers. Once mastered, this position can be easily changed to the traditional grip.

Special Helps

Teachers of young children have the opportunity to help children learn good writing habits from the start. Remind children frequently to check their sitting, paper, and pencil positions. Make the routine fun for children. Use a signal (such as a bell ringing) to let children know it's time to check their positions, or challenge them to zoom into a good writing position as quickly as they can. Finally, communicate with families by providing diagrams for using good writing positions at home.

It is important to understand that for most children the traditional tripod grip develops over time. Using a variety of activities that build hand skills will help. At the beginning of the writing session, name each finger (pinky, ring, etc.). As it is named, ask children to touch each finger to the thumb with their eyes open and then closed. Drawing, writing, and using manipulatives of all kinds will help children master the dual functions of the hand—using the index finger and thumb for prehension or precision movements, and the ring and pinky fingers for stabilizing.

—*Maureen King, O.T.R.*

Your Book

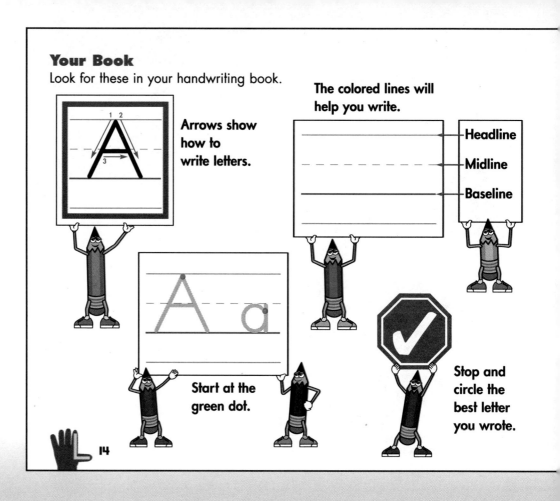

Your Book
Look for these in your handwriting book.

Arrows show how to write letters.

The colored lines will help you write.

Headline

Midline

Baseline

Start at the green dot.

Stop and circle the best letter you wrote.

14

Present the Activity

Direct children to look at the illustrations on student page 14. Help them recognize that there are four different sections on the page. This lesson will present each of the features in turn, providing opportunities for the children to search for examples of each one in subsequent pages in their books.

Model Box With Arrows

Point out the model box in the upper left part of student page 14. Ask children what letter is shown in the box. (**A**) Ask what else they notice in the model box. (*red arrows*) Explain that red arrows point in a certain direction and help them know which direction to write. When they begin to write letters, a model box will show them which letter they will write. Red arrows with numerals help them know how to write, starting with the first numeral and following the arrows.

Invite children to look at various pages in their books to find other examples of model boxes. Ask what is shown in each model box they find.

Guidelines

Have children look at the sample writing guidelines in the upper right part of the student page. Guide them in locating and naming each guideline. Have them name its color and tell whether the line is solid or broken.

Draw guidelines on the chalkboard and ask volunteers to name each line in the grid. Remind children that every stroke and every letter begin somewhere on these guidelines. Explain that using guidelines will help them write better letters.

Invite children to look through their pages to find examples of guidelines. Ask if the lines are colored the same way as in the model on student page 14.

Coaching Hint

Using Guidelines Distribute sheets of the lined writing paper children will be using in order to familiarize them with the guidelines. Help them locate the first set of guidelines. Demonstrate and have children follow along as you trace the headline with a blue crayon, the broken midline with blue, and the baseline with red. (visual, kinesthetic)

Fun and Games

auditory   visual   kinesthetic

Green Starting Dots

Have children look at the set of guidelines in the lower left corner of the student page. Point out the gray shaded letters. Explain that children will trace these letters throughout their books to help them learn how to write.

Point out the green dots on the shaded letters. Explain that these dots show them where to begin writing letters on the guidelines. When they start to trace or write, a green dot will help them know where to start.

Invite the children to look through their book to find other examples of shaded letters and green starting dots.

Stop and Check

Direct children to look on the student page and find the red stop sign with a check mark in it. Explain that this sign will appear on pages where the children write. It means they are to stop and look at the letters they have written and draw a circle around the best letter they wrote.

Invite the children to look through their book to find other examples of the Stop and Check sign.

Note: At the beginning of the year, children will vary in their ability to evaluate their own work. The development of self-evaluation skills is an important goal of handwriting instruction. Self-evaluation helps the children become independent learners.

Fun With Guidelines Draw guidelines with chalk on the playground hardtop or make them with masking tape on the classroom floor. Ask volunteers to follow directions similar to these:

> *Hop along the headline.*
> *Lie on the midline.*
> *Sit on the baseline.*
> *Sit in the space below the baseline.*
> *Walk the baseline on tiptoes.*

Invite children to say directions for classmates to follow. (auditory, visual, kinesthetic)

Walk the Line Place masking tape along the floor with a green dot at the beginning and a red dot at the end. Have the children walk the line, pretending to be walking a rail. (visual, kinesthetic)

You use vertical lines when you write.
Place your vertical strokes here.
Trace them with your finger.

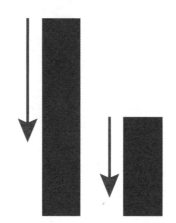

Find vertical lines in the picture.
Draw this picture or one of your own.

Using the Basic Strokes Pieces

It is suggested that you or an aide punch out the Basic Strokes pieces to prevent tearing. You may wish to laminate the pieces for year-long use. Alternately, you might use half the set now and save the remaining pieces for use later, when the first ones become worn out. Distribute a tall and a short blue vertical line to each child for the lesson. After the lesson, store the pieces in a zip-top bag for each child.

Present the Lines

Tell children that vertical lines are lines that stand up straight. Ask them to stand up straight. Point out that a vertical line might be drawn from the top of their heads to the bottom of their feet.

Help children find the blue vertical lines on student page 15. Have them use a tall and a short vertical stroke from their set of Basic Strokes pieces. Ask them to place the tall piece on top of the tall blue line on the student page. Then have them place the short piece on the short blue line.

Have students use their fingers to trace the pieces from top to bottom, following the direction of the arrows.

Model Have children watch as you pantomime pulling down a window shade. Ask them to guess what you are doing. Continue by pantomiming the erasing of vertical strokes on the chalkboard and unzipping a coat as you say, "Pull down straight." Have the children say the words as they do the actions with you.

Practice Let children use their Basic Strokes pieces in a variety of ways to explore vertical lines. Suggest that they hold the strokes against the chalkboard or chart paper and trace along one edge from top to bottom. Invite children to match their strokes to vertical lines they find in the classroom (e.g., along the door frame, on the classroom calendar).

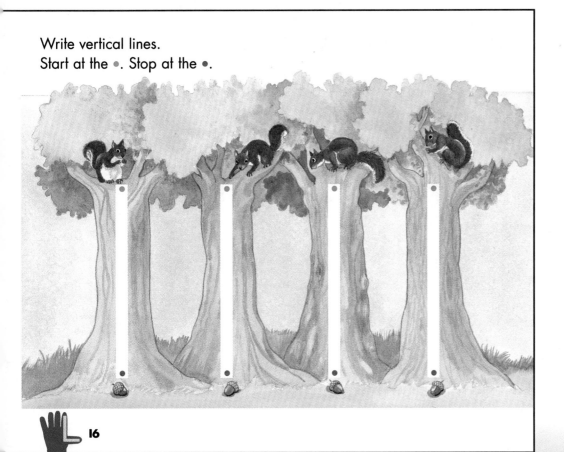

Write vertical lines.
Start at the •. Stop at the •.

16

Trace and Draw

Ask children to look at the picture of the lollipops. Help them identify the vertical lines in the picture. Have them use their index finger to trace each lollipop stick from top to bottom.

Point out the space for drawing on the student page. Direct the children to draw the lollipop picture, or a picture of their own, in this space. Remind them to draw vertical lines from top to bottom.

Invite children to share their completed drawings, pointing out the vertical lines.

Apply

Point out the tall trees on student page 16, and help children recognize the vertical space between the dots. Ask them to describe a line that would connect the dots on each tree trunk. (*straight up and down; vertical*)

Review the meaning of the green starting dots and the red stopping dots. Ask children to write vertical lines, beginning each one at the green dot and ending each at the red dot. Encourage children to write each stroke with a single, continuous movement.

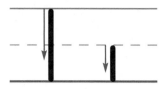

Pull down straight.

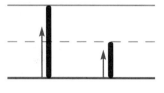

Push up straight.

Basic Strokes **Vertical Lines**

Write vertical lines.
Start at the •. Stop at the •.

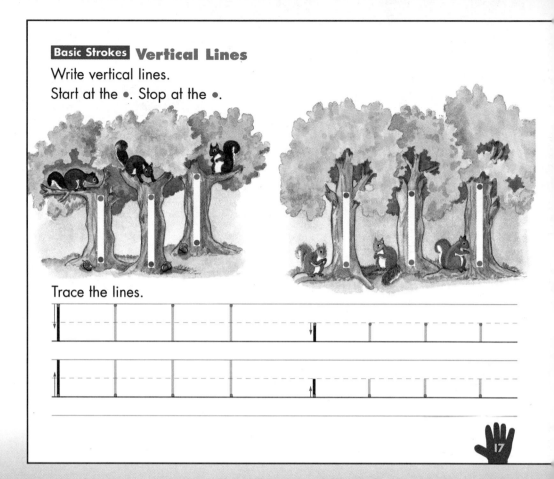

Trace the lines.

17

Present the Activity

Have children find the trees on student page 17 and notice the vertical space on each tree trunk. Make sure they notice the green starting dots and the red ending dots. Point out that on this page, some of the green dots appear at the bottom of the trees.

Ask children to write a vertical line on each tree trunk. Remind them to begin each line at the green starting dot and end at the red dot.

Model Model forming vertical lines in the air. Begin some at the top and say, "Pull down straight." Begin others at the bottom, saying "Push up straight." Have children repeat your words and follow the same actions.

Practice Let the children practice writing vertical strokes in centers or at their tables in a variety of ways: on marker boards or slates, on large paper at an easel, in sand or finger paint.

Trace and Evaluate

Point out the vertical lines on the guidelines at the bottom of student page 17. Help children recognize that the vertical lines in the first row begin at the headline or the midline and go down. Have them use a finger or a writing implement to trace each one, saying "Pull down straight" as they trace.

PRACTICE MASTERS 10–11

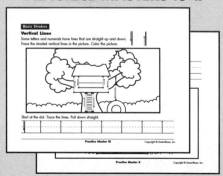

T16

Use your finger to trace the vertical lines in letters and numerals.

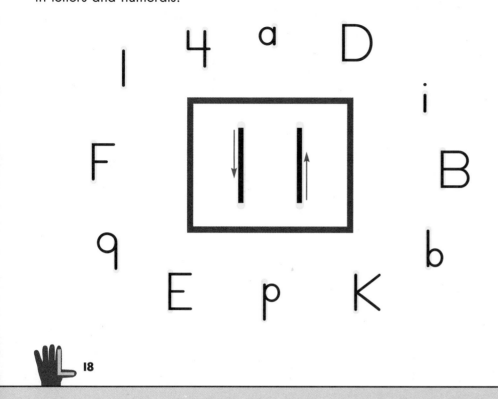

18

Basic Strokes To reinforce vertical strokes, make vertical lines with tape or chalk on the floor or on the hardtop area of the playground. Ask children to walk the line, placing one foot carefully in front of the other. Have them say, "Pull down straight" or "Push up straight" as they walk. (visual, auditory, kinesthetic)

Fun and Games

auditory   visual   kinesthetic

Lines to Trace Have the children trace top to bottom lines with thin white glue. Shake salt over the glue on the paper. When the glue and salt are dry, shake off the excess salt. The raised, textured lines can be used for touching from top to bottom and from bottom to top. (visual, kinesthetic)

Lines and Lines Distribute drawing paper and ask children to draw a picture with vertical lines. It could be somewhat like the picture on page 17 in their books. Provide crayons, markers, colored chalk, or paint. Have children discuss their lines with a partner and circle their longest and shortest lines. Encourage them to count the number of lines of a certain color and the total number of lines. (kinesthetic, visual, auditory)

Point out that the lines in the bottom row begin at the bottom and go up. Demonstrate by writing in the air and saying, "Push up straight." Encourage children to follow your model and say the words with you. Then ask them to trace the lines with a finger or a writing implement, saying "Push up straight."

To evaluate, observe whether children started and ended each line at the correct dots.

Apply

Direct the children to look at the letters and numerals on student page 18. Explain that the letters and numerals are arranged in a *web*. Ask them to think about vertical lines and to tell what they see in these examples. (*There is at least one vertical line in each.*)

Tell children to use their finger to trace the vertical lines they see. Point out the pull down straight and the push up straight models in the center of the page. Encourage children to say "Pull down straight" or "Push up straight" as they trace.

Using the Basic Strokes Pieces

It is suggested that you or an aide punch out the Basic Strokes pieces to prevent tearing. You may wish to laminate the pieces for year-long use. Alternately, you might use half the set now and save the remaining pieces for use later, when the first ones become worn out. Distribute a long and a short green horizontal line to each child for the lesson. After the lesson, add the pieces to each child's storage bag.

Basic Strokes **Horizontal Lines**

You use horizontal lines when you write. Place your horizontal strokes here. Trace them with your finger.

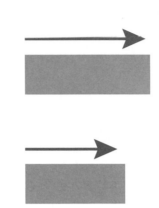

Find horizontal lines in the picture. Draw this picture or one of your own.

19

Present the Lines

Tell children that horizontal lines are lines that go straight across. Ask them to stand up and hold their arms out straight at the sides. Point out that a horizontal line might be drawn from one hand across to the other hand.

Help children find the green horizontal lines on student page 19. Have them use a long and a short horizontal stroke from their set of Basic Strokes pieces. Ask them to place the long piece on top of the long green line on the student page. Then have them place the short piece on the short green line.

Have children use their finger to trace the pieces from left to right, following the direction of the arrows.

Model Have the children watch as you pantomime pulling thread from a spool. Ask them to guess what you are doing. Continue by pantomiming pulling plastic wrap from its box and pulling the zipper on the top of a purse while you say "Slide right." Have the children say the words as they do the actions with you.

Practice Encourage children to find examples of horizontal lines in the classroom and, wherever possible, to use their finger to trace them from side to side. Suggest that children use the edge of a horizontal Basic Strokes piece as a stencil for making pictures on the chalkboard that contain horizontal lines.

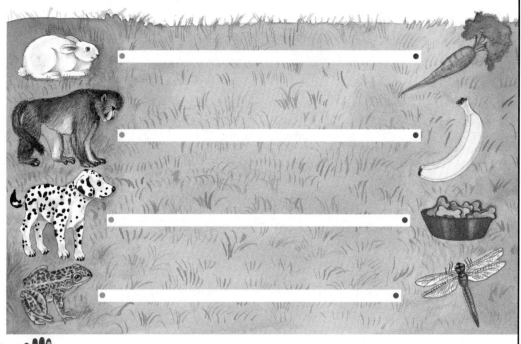

Write horizontal lines.
Start at the ●. Stop at the ●.

20

Trace and Draw

Ask children to look at the picture of the ladders. Help them identify the horizontal lines in the picture. Have them use their index finger to trace each horizontal rung from left to right.

Point out the space for drawing on the student page. Direct the children to draw the picture, or one of their own, in this space. Remind them to draw horizontal lines from left to right.

Invite children to share their completed drawings, pointing out the horizontal lines.

Apply

Point out the pathways on student page 20, and help children recognize the horizontal space between the dots. Ask them to describe a line that would connect the dots on each path. (*straight across; horizontal*)

Review the meaning of the green starting dots and the red stopping dots. Ask children to write horizontal lines, beginning each one at the green dot and ending each at the red dot. Encourage children to write each stroke with a single, continuous movement.

Slide right.

Slide left.

Basic Strokes **Horizontal Lines**
Write horizontal lines.
Start at the •. Stop at the •.

Trace the lines.

21

Present the Activity

Point out the animals and foods on student page 21, and help children notice the horizontal space between the dots. Make sure they notice the green starting dots and the red ending dots. Point out that on this page, some of the green dots appear at the right.

Ask children to write a horizontal line on each path. Remind them to begin each line at the green starting dot and end at the red dot.

Model Model forming horizontal lines in the air. Begin some at the left and say, "Slide right." Begin others at the right, saying "Slide left." Have children repeat your words and follow the same actions.

Practice Let the children practice writing horizontal strokes in centers or at their tables in a variety of ways: on marker boards or slates, on large paper at an easel, in sand or finger paint.

Trace and Evaluate

Point out the lines on the guidelines at the bottom of the page. Help children recognize that the horizontal lines in the first row begin at the left on either the midline, the baseline, or the headline and go right. Have them use a finger or a writing implement to trace each one, saying "Slide right."

PRACTICE MASTERS 12–13

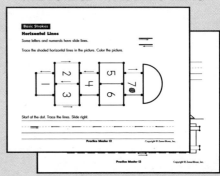

T20

Use your finger to trace the horizontal lines in letters and numerals.

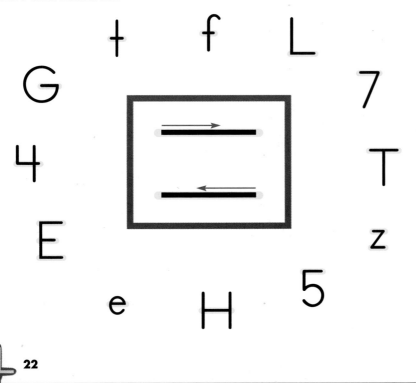

G   t   f   L

4   7   T

E   z

e   H   5

22

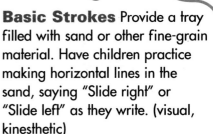

Coaching Hint

Basic Strokes Provide a tray filled with sand or other fine-grain material. Have children practice making horizontal lines in the sand, saying "Slide right" or "Slide left" as they write. (visual, kinesthetic)

Fun and Games

auditory   visual   kinesthetic

Apply

Point out that the lines in the bottom row begin at the right on the midline or the baseline, and go left. Demonstrate by writing in the air and saying, "Slide left." Encourage children to follow your model and say the words with you. Then ask them to trace the lines with a finger or a writing implement, saying "Slide left."

To evaluate, observe whether children started and ended each line at the correct dots.

Direct the children to look at the letters and numerals in the web on student page 22. Ask them to think about horizontal lines and to tell what they see in these examples. (*There is at least one horizontal line in each.*)

Tell children to use their finger to trace the horizontal lines they see. Point out the slide right and slide left models in the center of the page. Encourage children to say "Slide left" or "Slide right" as they trace.

Left to Right Place three objects in a row and ask the children to look at the left-to-right sequence. Mix up the objects and then have the children tell which object was first, second, and third. Repeat this activity using different shapes or colors of blocks or colored squares. You can increase the number of objects, depending on the ability of the children. (visual, auditory)

What's in a Name? Invite children to write their first name on the chalkboard (or if necessary, you write the names for them). Then encourage them to take turns finding horizontal lines in the letters in each other's names. Provide colored chalk, and have them highlight horizontal lines they see. (visual, kinesthetic)

Basic Strokes
Backward Circle Lines

Using the Basic Strokes Pieces

It is suggested that you or an aide punch out a large and a small red circle line and distribute them to each child for the lesson. After the lesson, add the pieces to each child's storage bag.

Basic Strokes **Backward Circle Lines**

You use backward circle lines when you write.
Place your circle strokes here.
Trace them with your finger.

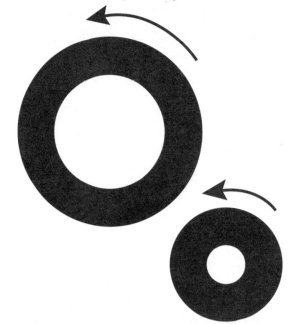

Find circle lines in the picture. Draw this picture or one of your own.

23

Present the Lines

Tell children that backward circle lines are lines that go around. Ask them to lean back with hands overhead and palms up to show a backward movement.

Help children find the red circle lines on student page 23. Have them use a small and a large circle from their set of Basic Strokes pieces. Ask them to place a small piece on top of the small red circle on the student page. Then have them do the same with a large piece on the large red circle.

Have children use their finger to trace the pieces in a backward circle motion, following the direction of the arrows.

Model Draw a ball on the chalkboard, beginning near the one o'clock position and forming a backward circle. Emphasize the starting point. Have the children draw a ball in the air using large muscle movements as you say, "Circle back all the way around."

Practice Encourage children to find examples of circle lines in the classroom and, wherever possible, to use their finger to trace some of them all the way around. Provide drawing materials and allow children to use their Basic Strokes pieces as stencils for drawing doughnuts, cars with wheels, faces, or other pictures that contain circle lines.

Write backward circle lines.
Start at the •. Stop at the •.

24

Trace and Draw

Ask children to look at the picture of the snowman. Help them identify the circle lines in the picture. Have them use their index finger to trace each snowman circle in a backward circle motion.

Point out the space for drawing on the student page. Direct the children to draw the picture, or one of their own, in this space. Remind them to begin each backward circle near the one o'clock position. Invite children to share their completed drawings, pointing out the circle lines.

Apply

Point out the flower garden on student page 24, and help children recognize the circular spaces around the flowers. Ask them to describe a line that would connect the dots on each space. (*circle*)

Review the meaning of the green starting dots and the red stopping dots. Ask children to write backward circle lines, beginning each one at the green dot and ending at the red dot. Encourage children to write each stroke with a smooth, continuous motion.

Basic Strokes
Backward Circle Lines

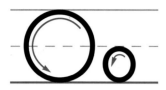

Circle back all the way around.

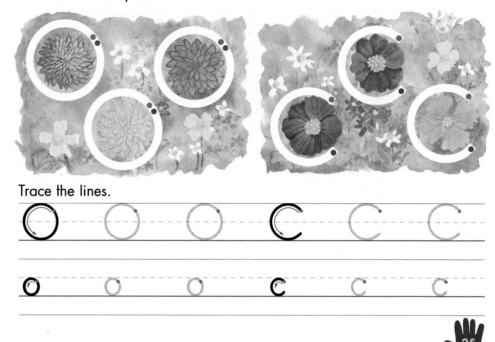

Basic Strokes **Backward Circle Lines**
Write backward circle lines.
Start at the ●. Stop at the ●.

Trace the lines.

25

Present the Activity

Have children find the flowers on student page 25 and notice the circle or partial circle around each flower. Make sure they notice the green starting dots and the red ending dots. Then ask them to write a backward circle or partial circle for each flower. Remind them to begin each circle at the green starting dot and end at the red dot.

Model Draw several backward circles on the chalkboard, beginning near the one o'clock position. As you make each circle, say, "Circle back all the way around." Direct the children to form backward circles in the air, repeating the stroke description as they move their hands. Ask several children to come to the chalkboard and trace over your circles with colored chalk.

Practice Let children practice writing backward circle strokes in centers or at their tables in a variety of ways: on marker boards or slates, on large paper at an easel, in sand or finger paint.

Trace and Evaluate

Point out the circles and partial circles at the bottom of the page. Help children recognize that the circles and partial circles in the first row are tall and the ones in the bottom row are short—that the shapes are the same except for size.

PRACTICE MASTERS 14–15

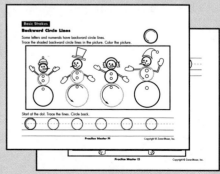

T24

Use your finger to trace the backward circle lines in letters and numerals.

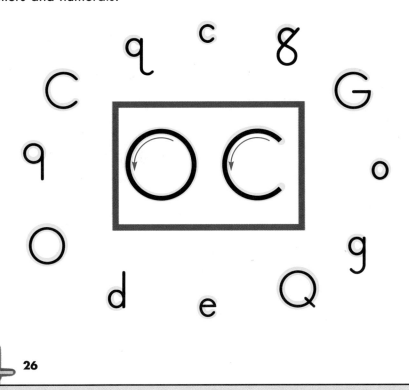

26

Basic Strokes Provide sewing cards that have holes punched in the shape of large or small circles. Encourage the children to use red yarn to "sew" the circles. (visual, kinesthetic)

Fun and Games

auditory   visual   kinesthetic

Circles and Circles Provide several circle stencils, markers, colored pencils, and crayons. Ask the children to trace the stencils, observing their hand movements occasionally to see that they are making the stroke properly. Encourage the children to complete their circles as they wish, by coloring them in, adding several circles on top to form a design, or making a picture by combining several circles. (visual, kinesthetic)

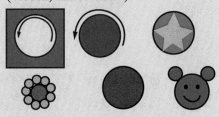

Circles Are Round Draw a large circle on a sheet of paper. Put a star for the start and an arrow pointing a direction for cutting. Duplicate a circle for each child. Have children cut out the circles. Talk about things that are round, and ask children to draw round things on their circles. (kinesthetic, auditory, visual)

Apply

Direct the children to look at the letters and numerals in the web on student page 26. Ask them to think about circles and to tell what they see in these examples. (*There is at least one circle or partial circle in each one.*)

Tell children to use their finger to trace the backward circle lines they see. Point out the backward circle models in the center of the page. Encourage children to say "Circle back all the way around" or "Circle back" as they trace.

Have children use a finger or a writing implement to trace each circle or partial circle. Demonstrate by writing in the air and saying "Circle back all the way around" or "Circle back." Encourage children to follow your model and say the words with you. Then ask them to trace the lines with a finger or a writing implement, saying the words as they trace.

To evaluate, observe whether children started and ended each circle at the correct dots.

Using the Basic Strokes Pieces

It is suggested that you or an aide punch out a tall and a short orange slant line and distribute them to each child for the lesson. After the lesson, add the pieces to each child's storage bag.

Basic Strokes **Slant Lines**

You use slant lines when you write. Place your slant strokes here. Trace them with your finger.

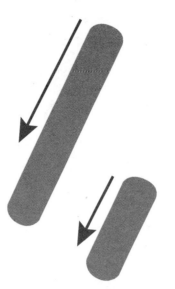

Find slant lines in the picture. Draw this picture or one of your own.

27

Present the Lines

Tell children that slant lines are lines that are tipped, or sloped. Ask children to hold their hands up, palms facing toward each other, and fingertips touching. Explain that their arms are making slants.

Help children find the orange slant lines on student page 27. Have them use a tall and a short slant piece from their set of Basic Strokes pieces. Ask them to place a tall piece on top of the tall orange line on the student page. Then have them do the same with a short piece on the short orange line. Have children use their finger to trace the pieces from top right to bottom left, following the direction of the arrows.

Model Have the children say the nursery rhyme "Jack and Jill" with you. Write a slant left stroke on the chalkboard while saying, "Slant left." Have the children say the rhyme again, and this time trace over the slant stroke when the children get to the falling down part of the rhyme. Ask the children to say the rhyme and trace the slant stroke in the air.

Practice Encourage children to find examples of slant lines in the classroom and, wherever possible, to match them with their Basic Strokes pieces and trace them with their fingers.

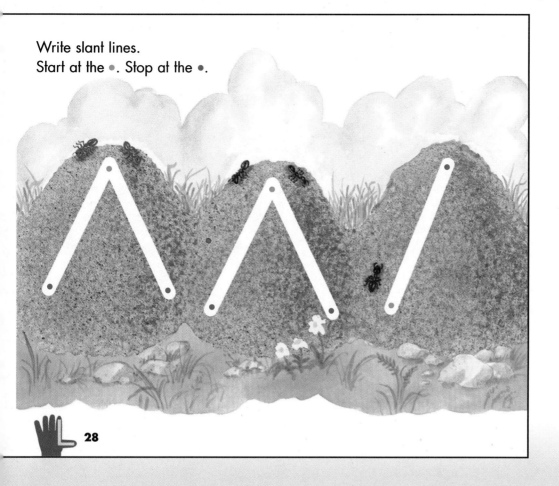

Write slant lines.
Start at the •. Stop at the •.

28

Trace and Draw

Ask children to look at the picture of the mountains. Help them identify slant lines in the picture. Have them use their index finger to trace each mountain slope.

Point out the space for drawing on the student page. Direct the children to draw the picture, or one of their own, in this space.

Invite children to share their completed drawings, pointing out the slant lines.

Apply

Point out the ants and anthills on student page 28, and help children recognize the slant spaces between the dots. Ask them to describe a line that would connect the dots on each ant path. (*slanted*)

Review the meaning of the green starting dots and the red stopping dots. Point out that on most of the ant hills the green dot is at the top, while on the last one it is at the bottom. Ask children to write slant lines, beginning each one at the green dot and ending at the red dot. Encourage children to write each stroke with a single, continuous line.

Slant
left.

Slant
right.

Slant
up.

Basic Strokes Slant Lines
Write slant lines.
Start at the •. Stop at the •.

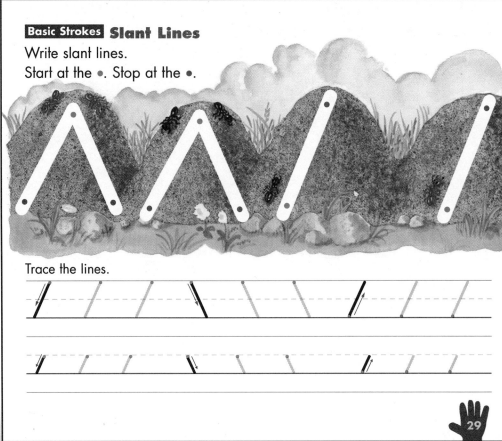

Trace the lines.

29

Present the Activity

Point out the anthills on student page 29, and help children recognize the slant space between the dots. Make sure they notice the green starting dots and the red ending dots. Then ask them to write a slant line on each anthill. Remind them to begin each line at the green starting dot and end at the red dot.

Model Model forming slant lines in the air. Begin some at the top and say, "Slant left" or "Slant right." Begin others at the bottom, saying, "Slant up." Have children repeat your words and follow the same actions.

Practice Let the children practice writing slant strokes in centers or at their tables in a variety of ways: on marker boards or slates, on large paper at an easel, in sand or finger paint.

Trace and Evaluate

Point out the lines on the guidelines at the bottom of the page. Help children recognize that the slant lines in the first row are tall, touching both the headline and the baseline. Have them use a finger or a writing implement to trace each one, saying "Slant left," "Slant right," or "Slant up" as they trace.

PRACTICE MASTERS 16–17

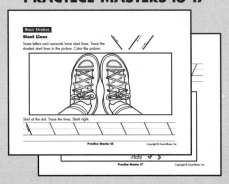

Use your finger to trace the slant lines in letters and numerals.

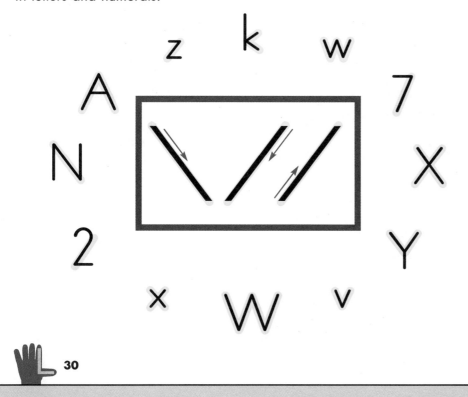

z   k   w

A

N   7

2   X

x   W   v   Y

W

👆 30

Coaching Hint

Basic Strokes Distribute laminated cards with at least two slant lines on them. Provide clay or fun dough and have children form short ropes to fit over the lines on the cards. (visual, kinesthetic)

Fun and Games

auditory   visual   kinesthetic

Apply

Point out that the lines in the bottom row touch the midline and the baseline. Direct the children to trace these lines, following the same procedure as with the tall slant lines.

To evaluate, observe whether the children started and ended at the correct dots.

Direct the children to look at the letters and numerals in the web on student page 30. Ask them to think about slant lines and to tell what they see in these examples. (*There is at least one slant line in each.*)

Tell children to use their finger to trace the slant lines they see. Point out the slant models in the center of the page. Encourage children to say "Slant left," "Slant right," or "Slant up" as they trace.

Draw Me a Picture Ask the children to go to the chalkboard and draw a picture of something with a slant line. (Picture cards might be handed to volunteers if the children are hesitant to think of ideas on their own.) As each child draws a picture, the other children may guess what is being drawn. Some examples are a sailboat, a swing set, a party hat, a pennant, a kite, and a house. (auditory, visual, kinesthetic)

Slant Lines Give the children pieces of paper with a large inverted **V** on them. Instruct the children to trace over the slant lines. Have them use these slant lines to make a picture. Some examples are a mountain, a clown with a pointed hat on, and a tepee. (visual, auditory, kinesthetic)

Using the Basic Strokes Pieces

It is suggested that you or an aide help the children select a large and a small red circle from their set of Basic Strokes pieces and have them ready for the lesson. After the lesson, return the pieces to each child's storage bag.

Basic Strokes **Forward Circle Lines**

You use forward circle lines when you write.
Place your circle strokes here.
Trace them with your finger.

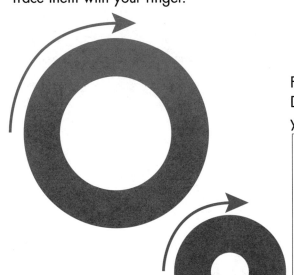

Find circle lines in the picture.
Draw this picture or one of
your own.

Present the Lines

Tell children that forward circle lines are round. Ask them to put their arms over their heads and then lean their head and arms forward to demonstrate circling forward.

Help children find the red circle lines on student page 31. Have them use a small and a large red circle from their set of Basic Strokes pieces. Ask them to place the small piece on top of the small circle on the page. Then have them do the same with a large circle on the large circle on the page.

Have children use their fingers to trace the pieces in a forward circle motion, following the direction of the arrows.

Model Have the children sing and move their hands with you as you sing *The wheels on the bus go round and round, round and round,* etc. Continue by pantomiming the forward turning motion of a wheel as you say, "Circle forward all the way around." Have the children say the words as they do the action with you.

Practice Encourage children to find examples of circle lines in the classroom and, wherever possible, to use their finger to trace them in a forward circle motion. Ask volunteers to use their Basic Strokes pieces as stencils to draw forward circles on chart paper. Have them mark the starting point for a forward circle—at about nine o'clock—with an **x**.

Write forward circle lines.
Start at the •. Stop at the •.

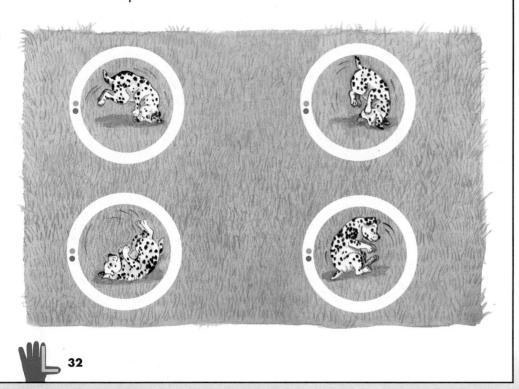

32

Trace and Draw

Ask children to look at the picture of the pizza. Help them identify the circles in the picture. Have them use their index finger to trace each in a forward circle motion.

Point out the space for drawing on the student page. Direct the children to draw the picture, or one of their own, in this space. Remind them to begin each forward circle at the nine o'clock position.

Invite children to share their completed drawings, pointing out the circle lines.

Apply

Point out the tumbling dogs on student page 32, and help children recognize the circular space around each dog. Ask them to describe a line that would connect the dots on each space. (*circle*)

Review the meaning of the green starting dots and the red stopping dots. Ask children to write forward circle lines, beginning each one at the green dot and ending at the red dot. Encourage children to write each stroke with a smooth, continuous motion.

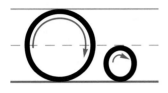

Circle forward.

Write forward circle lines.
Start at the •. Stop at the •.

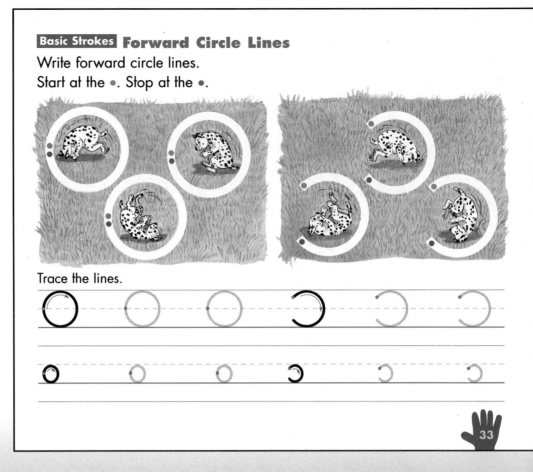

Trace the lines.

33

Present the Activity

Have children find the tumbling dogs on student page 33 and notice the circle or partial circle around each one. Make sure they notice the green starting dots and red ending dots. Then ask them to write forward circle lines, beginning each at the starting dot and ending at the red dot.

Model Model forming forward circles in the air. Make some circle forward all the way around, and make some circle part way as you say "Circle forward all the way around" and "Circle forward."

Practice Let the children practice writing forward circles in centers or at their tables in a variety of ways: on marker boards or slates, on large paper at an easel, in sand or finger paint.

Trace and Evaluate

Point out the circles and partial circles on the guidelines at the bottom of the page. Help children recognize that the circles and partial circles in the top row are tall and the ones in the bottom row are short—that the shapes are the same except for size.

PRACTICE MASTERS 18–19

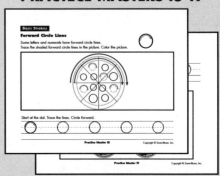

T32

Use your finger to trace the forward circle lines in letters and numerals.

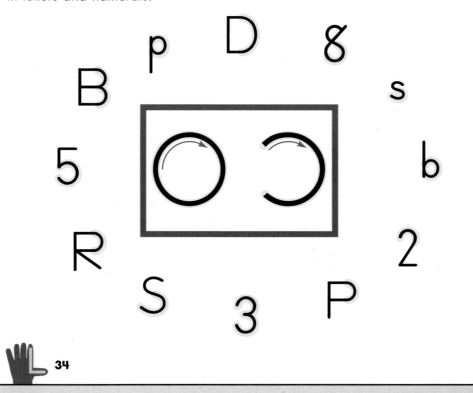

B p D 8
5 s
R b
S 3 P 2

34

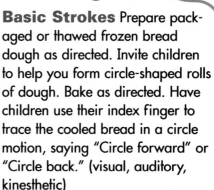
Fun and Games

auditory   visual   kinesthetic

Bubbles and Circles

Design a worksheet with a bubble wand and have the children trace around the forward circle bubbles. Say together the tongue twister *Bill blew a big bubble.* (visual, kinesthetic, auditory)

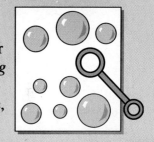

Circle Left, Circle Right

Invite children to join hands and form a circle. Review that a circle can go backward, to the left, or forward, to the right. Play some music and have the children move in a circle. Stop the music and have them change direction. Then chant this rhyme as you lead the children in following the words and circling around.

> *Circle left, circle left.*
> *Circle all around.*
> *Circle right, circle right.*
> *Stop and look around.*

(auditory, kinesthetic)

Apply

Have children use a finger or a writing implement to trace each circle or partial circle. Demonstrate by writing in the air and saying, "Circle forward all the way around" or "Circle forward." Encourage children to follow your model and say the words with you. Then ask them to trace the lines with a finger or a writing implement, saying the words as they trace.

To evaluate, observe whether children started and ended each line at the correct dots.

Direct the children to look at the web of letters and numerals on student page 34. Ask them to think about forward circle lines and to tell what they see in these examples. (*There is at least one circle or partial circle line in each.*)

Tell children to use their finger to trace the circle lines they see. Point out the forward circle models in the center of the page. Encourage children to say "Circle forward all the way around" or "Circle forward" as they trace.

Four Kinds of Lines

Before Writing

Write the four basic strokes, each on a separate piece of paper or tagboard (vertical, horizontal, circle, slant). Alternatively, use lines from a set of Basic Strokes pieces.

Show one stroke (circle) to the children and ask them to look around the room for objects that contain this stroke. Help the children by suggesting they look at the clock. Compare the circle on the paper to the clock in the classroom so the children can see the stroke in the object. Continue in the same manner with each of the remaining basic strokes.

Four Kinds of Lines
Use basic strokes to draw the picture frames.

35

Present the Activity

Direct children to look at the framed pictures of animals on student page 35. Encourage them to help you identify and say the name of each animal.

Ask the children what they notice about the frames around the pictures. Help them recognize that the frames are different shapes and that the shapes are made with various straight, slanted, or circle lines.

Write and Evaluate

Have the children write basic strokes, alone or in combination, to complete the picture frames. Encourage them to say appropriate descriptions, such as "Pull down straight," "Slant left," and "Circle forward all the way around" as they write.

Ask children to complete the kite pictures on student page 36 in the same way.

Check the hand and finger control of the children. Identify those children who need small-motor activities. Note those children who are having difficulty writing any of the basic strokes.

Coaching Hint

Find the Stroke Give each child a 9" x 12" piece of art or construction paper. Fold the paper in half. Name one basic stroke for the children to write in each section, using the back and front of the paper so all four strokes are included.

Have the children use the basic strokes to create pictures, using different colors so the basic stroke in each one remains obvious.

Use basic strokes to draw a line around each kite.

Coaching Hints

Tactile Letters Distribute individual boxes that contain narrow strips of felt and pieces of yarn. Have the children make different strokes with various colors of yarn. Then let them make pictures using the strips and basic strokes. (visual, kinesthetic)

Birdhouses Have the children fold drawing paper to make four boxes. Have them draw a triangular birdhouse in the first box and then continue with a rectangle, circle, and square. (auditory, visual, kinesthetic)

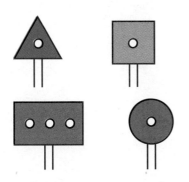

Drawing to Music Select and play lively, familiar songs as the children use crayons, markers, or paint and paintbrushes to draw basic strokes on construction paper, along with the music. If possible, have children take turns working at an easel as they draw. (auditory, kinesthetic)

Basic Strokes Use masking tape to make large shapes on the floor: square, rectangle, triangle, circle. Ask the children to walk, hop, or jump around each shape. Give specialized directions, such as "Slide your feet along a horizontal line," "Tip-toe along a vertical line," and "Walk like a crab around a circle line." (auditory, visual, kinesthetic)

Using the Basic Strokes Have the children take turns at the chalkboard as you give them directions for drawing parts of a house.

The outside walls should be drawn with tall vertical strokes; the baseline should be a slide right stroke; the windows are made with curve and horizontal strokes; the roof would be drawn with slant strokes; and the trees and bushes are made with circles.

Point to each part of the house, and ask the children to tell which stroke each part represents. Distribute unlined paper, and have the children draw their own pictures using the basic strokes. (visual, auditory, kinesthetic)

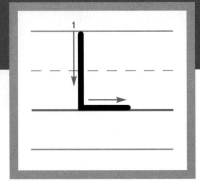

Touch the headline; **pull down straight** to the baseline. **Slide right**.

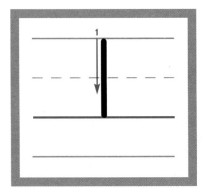

Touch the headline; **pull down straight** to the baseline.

Corrective Strategy

Demonstrate where to stop before making the slide right stroke. Remind children not to lift the pencil.

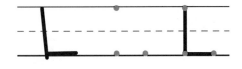

T36

Trace and write.

Lemonade Len Lisa

Stroke description to guide letter formation at home:
Pull down straight.
Slide right.

Directions: Discuss the picture on the page. Help children identify **L** in the word on the sign.

37

Use teaching steps 1, 2, and 3 below for pages 37 and 38 in the student book.

1. Present the Letter

Ask children to recognize the target letter in the ABC border and in the picture words. Focus attention on the letter's shape by asking what basic strokes it contains and what children think it resembles. (*L looks like the corner of a window or a picture frame.*)

Model Write the letter on guidelines as you say the stroke description. Have the children use the appropriate Basic Strokes pieces to form the letter on their desktop. Ask them to repeat the stroke description with you as they trace the letter on their desk.

Practice Let children practice writing the new letter in centers or at their tables in a variety of ways: on marker boards or slates, on large paper at an easel, in sand or finger paint.

2. Write and Evaluate

Ask children to trace the shaded letters with their finger or pencil, beginning each one at the dot. Then ask them to write a row of letters below the shaded models.

Stop and Check This icon directs children to stop and circle the best letter they wrote.

To help them evaluate **L,** ask:
• Does your **L** stop at the baseline before the slide right stroke?
• Is your slide right stroke near the baseline?

To help children evaluate **l,** ask:
• Does your **l** begin near the headline?
• Is your **l** straight up and down?

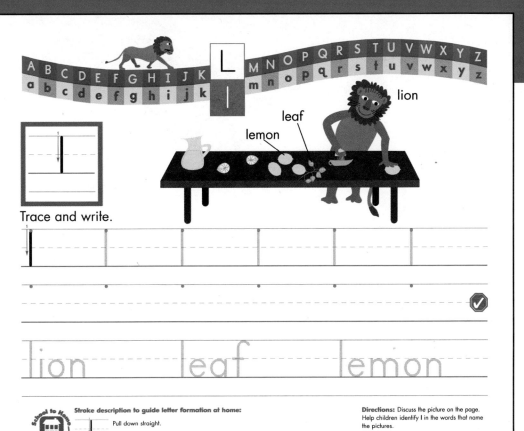

lion

leaf

lemon

Trace and write.

lion   leaf   lemon

Stroke description to guide letter formation at home:

Pull down straight.

Directions: Discuss the picture on the page. Help children identify l in the words that name the pictures.

PRACTICE MASTER 20

Trace and write.

Practice Master 20   Copyright © Zaner-Bloser, Inc.

PRACTICE MASTER 21

Trace and write.

Practice Master 21   Copyright © Zaner-Bloser, Inc.

---

3 Apply

Ask children to trace the target letter in each shaded word with their finger or pencil. Children who are ready may trace the complete words. Relate the words to the picture at the top of the page.

School to Home

Families may use the stroke descriptions on the student page to encourage good letter formation at home. Copy and distribute **Practice Master 83** for children to take home for more practice.

Fun and Games

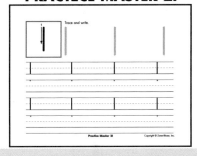

auditory   visual   kinesthetic

Using Manipulatives Have the children use small, round sponges to print a row of circles across the middle of a piece of construction paper. When the paint dries, have them add the eyes, mouth, feelers, and L-shaped legs with crayon or marker to make a caterpillar. (kinesthetic, visual)

Shadow Letters Turn on the light of a filmstrip projector or a good flashlight and let the children take turns making **L** shadows with their hands. (visual, kinesthetic)

Phonics Connection

Provide circles of construction paper and craft sticks. Show how to glue them together to make lollipops. Have each child write l on his or her lollipop. Say groups of words such as *man, lion, tall*. Ask children to hold up their lollipops each time they hear the /l/ sound at the beginning of a word. (auditory, visual, kinesthetic)

T37

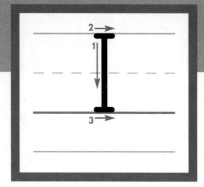

Touch the headline; **pull down straight** to the baseline. Lift. Touch the headline; **slide right**. Lift. Touch the baseline; **slide right**.

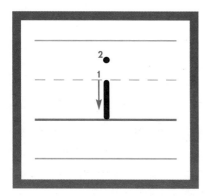

Touch the midline; **pull down straight** to the baseline. Lift. **Dot.**

Corrective Strategy

Have children trace the pull down straight stroke and then connect dots placed at appropriate widths on the headline and baseline. Say the description as they write.

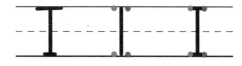

T38

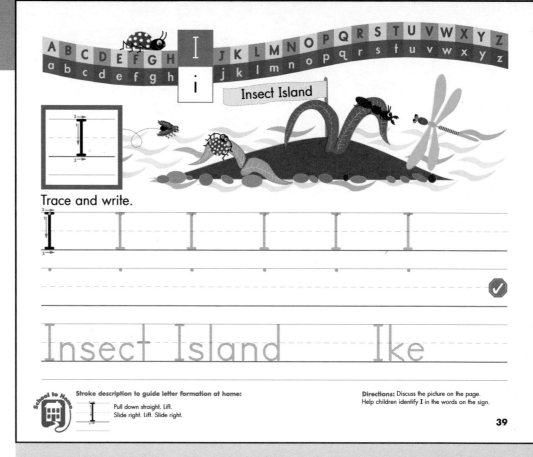

Insect Island

Trace and write.

Insect Island   Ike

School to Home

Stroke description to guide letter formation at home:

Pull down straight. Lift.
Slide right. Lift. Slide right.

Directions: Discuss the picture on the page. Help children identify **I** in the words on the sign.

39

Use teaching steps 1, 2, and 3 below for pages 39 and 40 in the student book.

1. Present the Letter

Ask children to recognize the target letter in the ABC border and in the picture words. Have the children look at uppercase **I**. Ask volunteers to help you describe how the two slide right strokes are alike. (*They are the same width.*)

Model Write the letter on guidelines as you say the stroke description. Guide the children in using the appropriate Basic Strokes pieces to form **I** on their desk. Have them say the description with you as they trace the shape with their finger.

Practice Let children practice writing the new letter in centers or at their tables in a variety of ways: on marker boards or slates, on large paper at an easel, in sand or finger paint.

2. Write and Evaluate

Ask children to trace the shaded letters with their finger or pencil, beginning each one at the dot. Then ask them to write a row of letters below the shaded models.

Stop and Check This icon directs children to stop and circle the best letter they wrote.

To help them evaluate **I,** ask:
- Does your **I** begin near the headline?
- Is your **I** not too skinny or too fat?

To help children evaluate **i,** ask:
- Is your **i** resting on the baseline?
- Is your letter straight up and down?

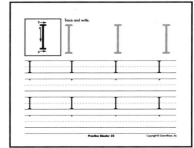

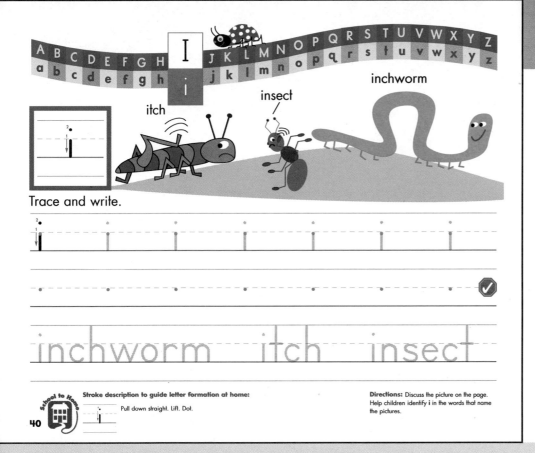

Trace and write.

inchworm   itch   insect

Directions: Discuss the picture on the page. Help children identify **i** in the words that name the pictures.

PRACTICE MASTER 22

Trace and write.

PRACTICE MASTER 23

Trace and write.

---

③ Apply

Ask children to trace the target letter in each shaded word with their finger or pencil. Children who are ready may trace the complete words. Relate the words to the picture at the top of the page.

School to Home

Families may use the stroke descriptions on the student page to encourage good letter formation at home. Copy and distribute **Practice Master 84** for children to take home for more practice.

Readiness Counts!

Letter Shape

Young children may have difficulty recognizing specific aspects of a letter's shape. Use the following activities in your classroom to develop shape concepts. (See page T7 for characteristics of the pre-writer, the emergent writer, and the developing writer.)

For the Pre-Writer
Have the children play this game in small groups. Whisper the name of a letter to one group. Have the children in that group use their bodies to form the letter. Encourage them to work as a team. Some children might lie on the floor to make the shape as other children help direct the pose. Encourage each group to take a turn at forming letters.

For the Emergent Writer
Write a letter on a piece of paper and display it in a place where children can easily see it. Ask children to describe the way the letter looks. For example, an **L** could be described as having three points, having two lines, looking like the corner of a window or a doorway, and so on.

For the Developing Writer
Invite several children to dip paintbrushes in water and make water marks on the chalkboard. Use the stroke descriptions, such as "pull down straight" or "slide right" to encourage the children to develop proper writing strokes.

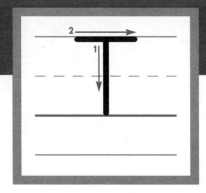

Touch the headline; **pull down straight** to the baseline. Lift. Touch the headline; **slide right**.

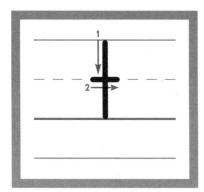

Touch the headline; **pull down straight** to the baseline. Lift. Touch the midline; **slide right**.

Corrective Strategy

Place dots to show children the width of the slide right stroke.

T40

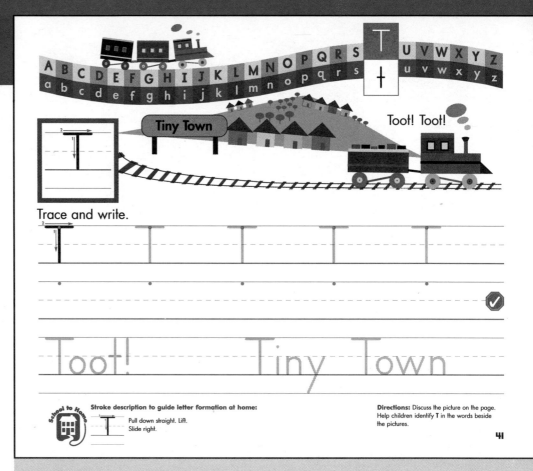

Trace and write.

Toot!   Tiny Town

School to Home

Stroke description to guide letter formation at home:

Pull down straight. Lift.
Slide right.

Directions: Discuss the picture on the page. Help children identify **T** in the words beside the pictures.

41

Use teaching steps 1, 2, and 3 below for pages 41 and 42 in the student book.

1. Present the Letter

Ask children to recognize the target letter in the ABC border and in the picture words. Talk about what basic strokes **T** contains and what children think it resembles.

Model Dip your index finger in a container of water and write **T** on guidelines on the chalkboard as you say the stroke description. Encourage children to take turns dipping their finger in water and writing **T** on the chalkboard, repeating the stroke description with you as they write.

Practice Let children practice writing the new letter in centers or at their tables in a variety of ways: on marker boards or slates, on large paper at an easel, in sand or finger paint.

2. Write and Evaluate

Ask children to trace the shaded letters with their finger or pencil, beginning each one at the dot. Then ask them to write a row of letters below the shaded models.

Stop and Check This icon directs children to stop and circle the best letter they wrote.

To help them evaluate **T,** ask:
- Is your slide right stroke near the headline?
- Is your **T** about the same size as the model?

To help children evaluate **t,** ask:
- Is your **t** straight up and down?
- Is the slide right stroke written near the midline?

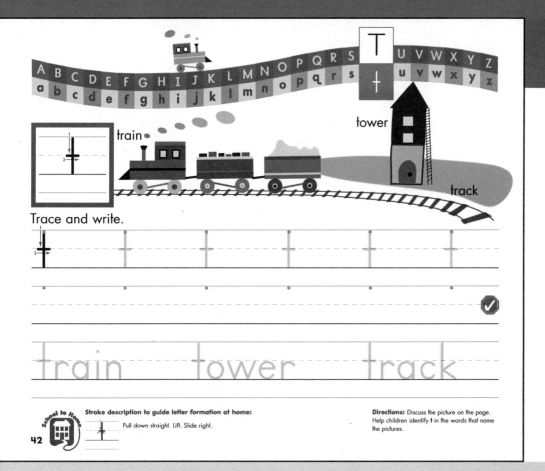

train

tower

track

Trace and write.

train   tower   track

Stroke description to guide letter formation at home:
Pull down straight. Lift. Slide right.

Directions: Discuss the picture on the page. Help children identify **t** in the words that name the pictures.

PRACTICE MASTER 24

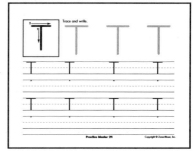

Trace and write.

PRACTICE MASTER 25

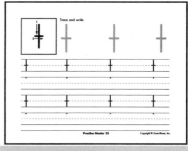

Trace and write.

Apply

Ask children to trace the target letter in each shaded word with their finger or pencil. Children who are ready may trace the complete words. Relate the words to the picture at the top of the page.

Families may use the stroke descriptions on the student page to encourage good letter formation at home. Copy and distribute **Practice Master 85** for children to take home for more practice.

Fun and Games

 auditory   visual   kinesthetic

Using Manipulatives Give out drawing paper and crayons or markers. Ask the children to close their eyes and imagine an animal story character named Tai. Tell the children to open their eyes and use the writing utensils to draw the animal character they pictured. Provide glue and a variety of small objects, such as buttons, small scraps of paper, and pieces of yarn or ribbon. Have children use them to add features to their drawing. (kinesthetic, visual)

Hokey-Pokey To help the children practice directionality and basic handwriting strokes, sing the words with the children, and act out the movements directed in each line.

Put your right hand in.
Put your right hand out.
Put your right hand in,
And you shake it all about.
You slide to the right
And you slide to the left
And that's how we play our
*   game!*
(auditory, kinesthetic)

Phonics Connection

Draw children's attention to your daily message chart. Choose a letter and help children recognize its sound, e.g., /t/ for the letter **t**. Ask one child to find and mark it on the chart and say its sound. Invite individual children to find that letter in other words on the chart, saying its sound and then pronouncing the entire word, if possible. (visual, kinesthetic)

Practice

auditory   visual   kinesthetic

Practice is critical to handwriting success. Each child benefits most from brief periods of practice done in his or her dominant learning modality. Practice activities that provide meaningful purposes for writing are best. Try these suggestions.

- In a center, provide models of short notes to family members, friends, or book characters. Ask children to use the models to write notes on colored paper or old greeting cards.

- Work together to create rhymes and songs that describe how to write letters. Here is an example for the letter **i**: *To make me, write a short line down. Then, guess what I've got. A dot!* Have volunteers perform the songs for the class and sing them as they practice writing their letters.

- Cut letters from sandpaper. Ask children to trace them with their fingers, following the correct stroke sequence.

T42

Practice

Write the letters.

43

---

1. Review the Letters

Write the letters **L, l, I, i,** and **T, t** on the chalkboard or chart paper. Invite a volunteer to come up and trace each letter you wrote as you repeat its stroke description. Next, give clues that describe one of the letters, such as *This letter is tall. It wears a hat. It has a slide right line on top.* Invite children to guess the letter. (*T*) Repeat for several more letters.

2. Write and Evaluate

Remind children to check their sitting, paper, and pencil positions. Point out that there are no green starting dots on the page. Ask children if they remember where to begin each letter. Then have them complete student page 43. If time allows, challenge the children to write words that name the pictures on the page.

✓ **Stop and Check** Praise children's progress in writing these letters. Invite volunteers to tell how their writing has improved. To help children evaluate their letters, ask:

- Did you pull down straight?
- Did you dot your **i**?
- Did you cross **t** near the midline?
- Is your **I** not too skinny or too fat—about the same width as the model?

Write the Alphabet

Write the missing uppercase letters.

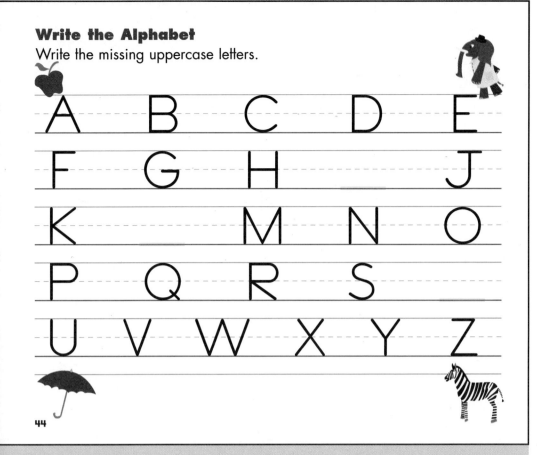

A B C D E
F G H J
K M N O
P Q R S
U V W X Y Z

44

Write the Alphabet pages show-case children's ability to write letters from memory. When children write a letter automatically, beginning at the correct starting point and using the correct stroke sequence, they demonstrate that they have successfully formed a clear mental and motor image of the letter.

 **Using Manipulatives**

Using manipulatives during handwriting instruction allows children to see, touch, and demonstrate the way letters are formed. Try some of the following ideas for hands-on handwriting in your classroom.

- Provide Zaner-Bloser *Touch and Trace Letter Cards* for letter practice.
- Create a "letter town" with letter-shaped block buildings.
- Touch and trace large magnetic letters.
- Use tagboard and a hole punch to make a sewing card for each letter. Provide shoelaces for lacing.
- Challenge children to form letter shapes from rows of dry beans, buttons, counting bears, craft sticks, or other small pieces.
- Provide a variety of writing tools that interest and motivate children, including chalk, scented markers, glitter glue pens, magic slates, and sheets of newsprint.

 **Apply**

Sing "The Alphabet Song" with children. Ask them to clap or stand up when they hear **L, I,** or **T.** You may wish to box or high-light the letters on an uppercase alphabet chart you have prepared. Save the chart for use with subsequent *Write the Alphabet* pages.

Examine student page 44 with the children. Point out that there are no models on the page. Tell children they can show that they really know how to write their letters when they can write them "by heart."

Ask children to complete the page on their own, writing the missing uppercase letters within the alphabet. Observe whether children are writing these letters automatically and correctly. Celebrate their accomplishment!

Special Helps

To reinforce concepts of left-to-right and top-to-bottom, involve children in making practice sheets. Have children place stickers across the top of a sheet of paper and the same number across the bottom. Have them draw lines to con-nect the stickers.

Similarly, have children con-nect stickers from the left side of a page to the right side. This encourages children to cross the midline of their bodies with the writing hand—an important handwrit-ing skill. For children who struggle with directionality, create a folder of laminated practice sheets for ongoing reinforcement.

—*Maureen King, O.T.R.*

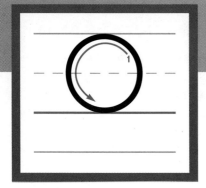

Touch below the headline; **circle back** (left) all the way around.

Touch below the midline; **circle back** (left) all the way around.

Corrective Strategy

To help children close **O**, place dots to help them write while you say the stroke description.

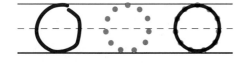

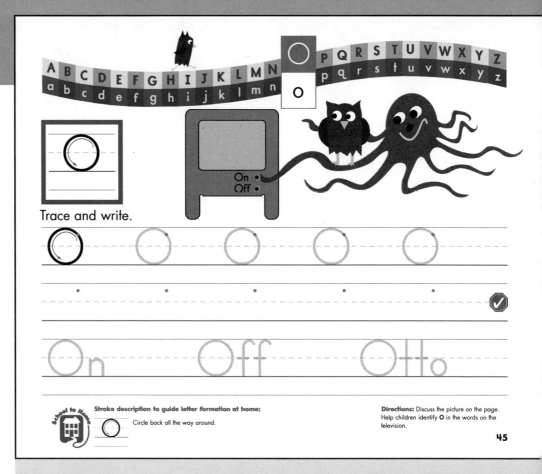

Trace and write.

Stroke description to guide letter formation at home:
Circle back all the way around.

Directions: Discuss the picture on the page. Help children identify **O** in the words on the television.

45

Use teaching steps 1, 2, and 3 below for pages 45 and 46 in the student book.

1. Present the Letter

Ask children to recognize the target letter in the ABC border and in the picture words. Then have them name things in the classroom that look like the letter **O**. (*clock, circular trash can, letters in environmental print*)

Model Write the letter on guidelines as you say the stroke description. Give children circular carton lids and have them trace the outer edge of the lid with their finger as you say the description. Show them where to begin and in which direction to circle.

Practice Let children practice writing the new letter in centers or at their tables in a variety of ways: on marker boards or slates, on large paper at an easel, in sand or finger paint.

2. Write and Evaluate

Ask children to trace the shaded letters with their finger or pencil, beginning each one at the dot. Then ask them to write a row of letters below the shaded models.

Stop and Check This icon directs children to stop and circle the best letter they wrote.

To help them evaluate **O,** ask:
• Is your **O** closed?
• Is your **O** about the same size as the model?

To help children evaluate **o,** ask:
• Is your **o** round?
• Does your **o** rest on the baseline?

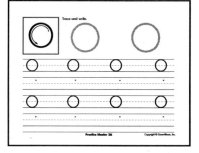

PRACTICE MASTER 26

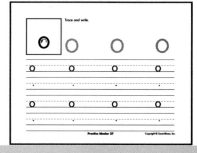

PRACTICE MASTER 27

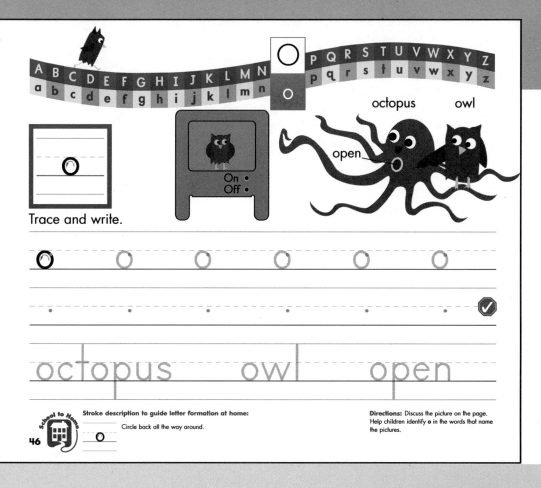

Trace and write.

octopus   owl

open

octopus   owl   open

Directions: Discuss the picture on the page. Help children identify **o** in the words that name the pictures.

---

③ Apply

Ask children to trace the target letter in each shaded word with their finger or pencil. Children who are ready may trace the complete words. Relate the words to the picture at the top of the page.

School to Home

Families may use the stroke descriptions on the student page to encourage good letter formation at home. Copy and distribute **Practice Master 86** for children to take home for more practice.

Readiness Counts!

Left-Handed Writers

If a child is definitely left-handed, teach him or her to write with that hand. If hand preference is not clear, observe the child in a variety of activities: playing with a hand puppet, putting pegs in a pegboard, throwing a ball, holding a spoon, and cutting with scissors. If a child is truly ambidextrous, it is probably best to train the right hand. (See page T7 for characteristics of the pre-writer, the emergent writer, and the developing writer.)

For the Pre-Writer

Allow the left-hander to practice free, full arm movement by writing on the chalkboard. At about face level, make pairs of dots about six inches apart vertically and have

the child connect them. Learning to make straight lines will facilitate legibility when the child writes.

For the Emergent Writer

Show the left-hander how to hold the pencil a little higher than the right-hander—well above the raw wood. This will enable the child to see the writing more easily and prevent the need for the child to adopt inefficient writing positions. The Zaner-Bloser *Writing Frame* fosters correct hand position because the hand holding the pencil and resting over the frame automatically settles into the correct position.

For the Developing Writer

Left-handers may twist or hook the hand or wrist in an attempt to see the paper. Discourage the hooked-wrist writing position by modeling correct paper placement for the left-hander. (See page T10 for more information.)

Touch the headline; **slant left** to the baseline. Lift. Touch the headline; **slant right** to the baseline. Lift. Touch the midline; **slide right**.

Touch below the midline; **circle back** (left) all the way around. **Push up straight** to the midline. **Pull down straight** to the baseline.

Alternate Letter Formation

Use this stroke description to show an alternate method for children who have difficulty using the continuous-stroke method.

   Circle back all the way around. Lift. **Pull down straight**.

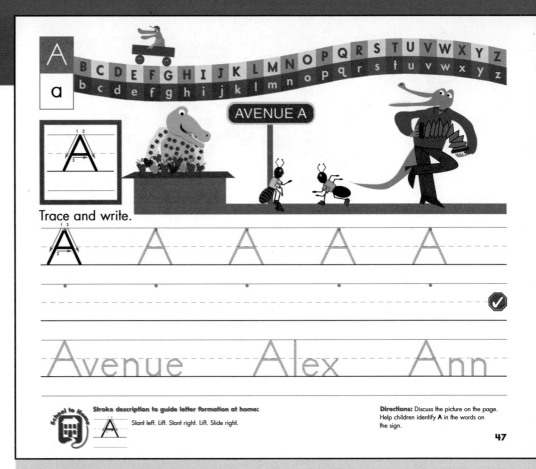

Trace and write.

AVENUE A

Avenue   Alex   Ann

Stroke description to guide letter formation at home:

A Slant left. Lift. Slant right. Lift. Slide right.

Directions: Discuss the picture on the page. Help children identify **A** in the words on the sign.

47

Use teaching steps 1, 2, and 3 below for pages 47 and 48 in the student book.

1. Present the Letter

Ask children to recognize the target letter in the ABC border and in the picture words. Have them look at **A,** and help them identify the strokes that make the letter. (*slant left, slant right, slide right*)

Model Write the letter on guidelines as you say the stroke description. Guide the children in using the appropriate Basic Strokes pieces to form **A** on their desk. Have them say the description with you as they trace the shape with their finger.

Practice Let children practice writing the new letter in centers or at their tables in a variety of ways: on marker boards or slates, on large paper at an easel, in sand or finger paint.

2. Write and Evaluate

Ask children to trace the shaded letters with their finger or pencil, beginning each one at the dot. Then ask them to write a row of letters below the shaded models.

Stop and Check This icon directs children to stop and circle the best letter they wrote.

To help them evaluate **A,** ask:
• Is your slide right stroke near the midline?
• Do your slant strokes touch the headline at about the same spot?

To help children evaluate **a,** ask:
• Is your circle round?
• Does the vertical line touch the circle?

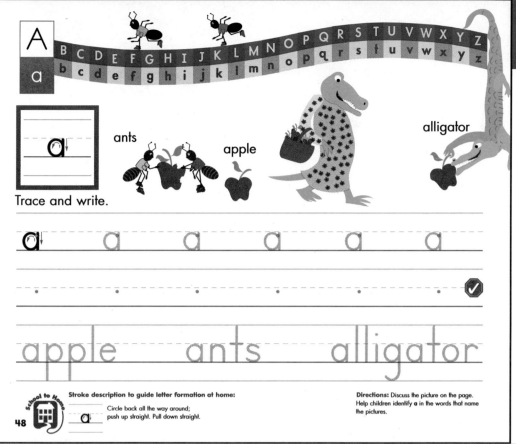

A a
B C D E F G H I J K L M N O P Q R S T U V W X Y Z
a b c d e f g h i j k l m n o p q r s t u v w x y z

ants
apple
alligator

a

Trace and write.

a   a   a   a   a   a

apple   ants   alligator

Directions: Discuss the picture on the page. Help children identify **a** in the words that name the pictures.

Aa

PRACTICE MASTER 28

Trace and write.
A   A   A
A   A   A   A
A   A   A   A

Practice Master 28   Copyright © Zaner-Bloser, Inc.

PRACTICE MASTER 29

Trace and write.
a   a   a   a
a   a   a   a
a   a   a   a

Practice Master 29   Copyright © Zaner-Bloser, Inc.

---

3 Apply

Ask children to trace the target letter in each shaded word with their finger or pencil. Children who are ready may trace the complete words. Relate the words to the picture at the top of the page.

Fun and Games

auditory   visual   kinesthetic

Using Manipulatives
Provide pieces of sponge cut in the shape of the target letter. Have children use the sponge to make the letter with water on the chalkboard. Ask them to name the letter and repeat the stroke description for forming the letter as they watch the letter disappear. (visual, kinesthetic)

Simon Says Play the traditional game of "Simon Says," but use words that relate to writing. Directions such as "Simon says slide right; Simon says slide left; Circle forward" help children understand the terms they are using as they learn to write. (kinesthetic, auditory)

Phonics Connection

Prepare a tray of wet sand or shaving cream on a table. Tell children to listen for words that begin with the first sound they hear in *alligator*. Then say words such as *ask, avenue, apple, dog, tree, ant,* and *ax.* Tell children to write **a** in the sand or shaving cream if the word begins like *alligator*. (auditory, kinesthetic, visual)

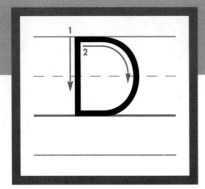

Touch the headline; **pull down straight** to the baseline. Lift. Touch the headline; **Slide right; curve forward** (right) to the baseline; **slide left**.

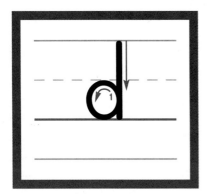

Touch below the midline; **circle back** (left) all the way around. **Push up straight** to the headline. **Pull down straight** to the baseline.

Alternate Letter Formation

Use this stroke description to show an alternate method for children who have difficulty using the continuous-stroke method.

 Circle back all the way around. Lift. **Pull down straight**.

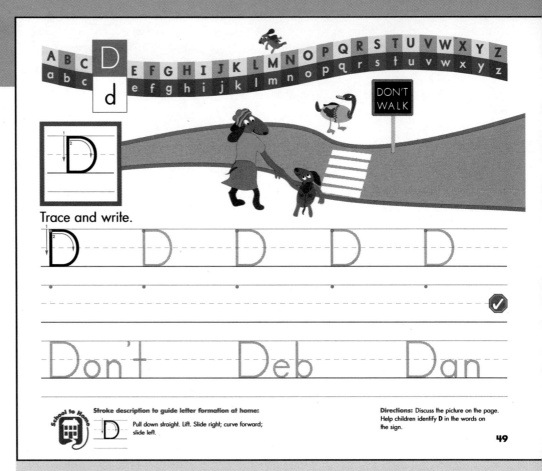

Trace and write.

Stroke description to guide letter formation at home:

Pull down straight. Lift. Slide right; curve forward; slide left.

Directions: Discuss the picture on the page. Help children identify **D** in the words on the sign.

49

Use teaching steps 1, 2, and 3 below for pages 49 and 50 in the student book.

1. Present the Letter

Ask children to recognize the target letter in the ABC border and in the picture words. Then have them look at the letter as you discuss its shape and attributes. Talk about the basic strokes it contains. (*vertical, slide right, curve forward, slide left*)

Model Write the letter on guidelines as you say the stroke description. Model writing it in the air as you repeat the stroke description. Have the children say it as they write the letter in the air with you.

Practice Let children practice writing the new letter in centers or at their tables in a variety of ways: on marker boards or slates, on large paper at an easel, in sand or finger paint.

2. Write and Evaluate

Ask children to trace the shaded letters with their finger or pencil, beginning each one at the dot. Then ask them to write a row of letters below the shaded models.

Stop and Check This icon directs children to stop and circle the best letter they wrote.

To help them evaluate **D,** ask:
• Is your vertical stroke straight?
• Does your **D** curve at the right place?

To help children evaluate **d,** ask:
• Does your **d** touch the headline?
• Is your circle round?

T48

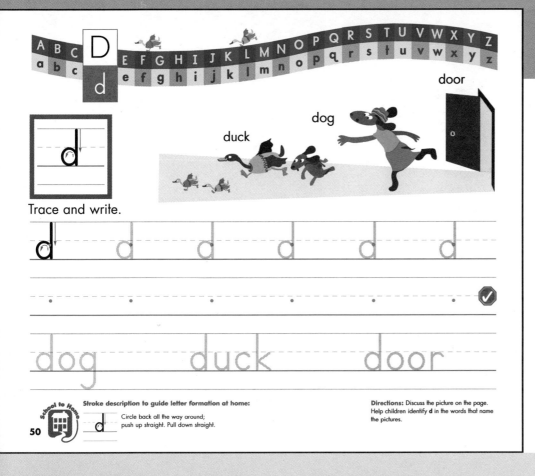

Dd

Trace and write.

d

dog   duck   door

Stroke description to guide letter formation at home:

d Circle back all the way around;
push up straight. Pull down straight.

Directions: Discuss the picture on the page.
Help children identify **d** in the words that name
the pictures.

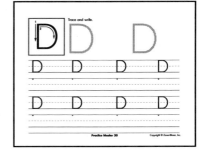

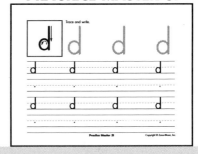

Apply

Ask children to trace the target letter in each shaded word with their finger or pencil. Children who are ready may trace the complete words. Relate the words to the picture at the top of the page.

Families may use the stroke descriptions on the student page to encourage good letter formation at home. Copy and distribute **Practice Master 88** for children to take home for more practice.

Readiness Counts!

Fine Motor Skills

A child's lack of fine-motor development may remain somewhat hidden until the child experiences difficulties with such common actions as using scissors or handwriting. Use the following activities in your classroom to develop fine-motor skills. (See page T7 for characteristics of the pre-writer, the emergent writer, and the developing writer.)

For the Pre-Writer

Winding up a toy, pouring something from one container into a hand-held container, using a hammer and nails or a screwdriver and screws all are examples of actions that help a child strengthen a sense of dominant and recessive hand.

For the Emergent Writer

If a child makes vertical, jagged lines when attempting to make small, circular movements, provide small handfuls of clay or similar material and tell the child to roll them, one by one, between the curved palms of the hands to make smooth ball shapes similar to meatballs.

For the Developing Writer

If the child holds a writing implement in a palm/fist grasp, have the child use his or her thumb and fingertips to rotate a jar lid or similar disk as it lies on a table surface. As the child gains expertise, have him or her do the same motion, rotating the disk in the air with the palm facing up.

Practice

auditory visual kinesthetic

Practice is critical to handwriting success. Each child benefits most from brief periods of practice done in his or her dominant learning modality. Too much practice of letters in isolation is frustrating for most children and promotes sloppy writing. Instead, try these suggestions.

- Ask children to write the target letter 3–4 times, using their best handwriting. Then show them how to fold the top of the paper down and back, right above their writing, so their letters can be held directly under the models in the handwriting book for comparison. Ask children to circle their best letter and tell why it is the best.

- After a child writes a letter 3–4 times, encourage him or her to discuss the letters with you to decide which one is best. For example, say, "I notice that your second letter has a nice round circle. What do you notice?"

- Provide cups of water and paintbrushes. Ask children to use the water to write the target letter 3–4 times in a large size on a chalkboard or slate. When they have decided which letter they wrote is best, they may trace it with chalk.

Write the letters.

o   o   a   a   d   d

O   O   A   A   D   D

1. Review the Letters

Write the letters **O, o, A, a,** and **D, d** on the chalkboard or chart paper. Invite a volunteer to come up and trace each letter you wrote as you repeat its stroke description. Next, give clues that describe one of the letters, such as *This letter is a short circle. It rolls along beside its parent.* Invite children to guess the letter. (*o*) Repeat for several more letters.

2. Write and Evaluate

Remind children to check their sitting, paper, and pencil positions. Point out that there are no green starting dots on the page. Ask children if they remember where to begin each letter. Then have them complete student page 51. If time allows, challenge the children to write words that name the pictures on the page.

✓ **Stop and Check** Praise children's progress in writing these letters. Invite volunteers to tell how their writing has improved. To help children evaluate their letters, ask:

- Does your vertical line touch your circle line in **a**?
- Is your uppercase **O** tall? Is your lowercase **o** short?
- Did you retrace smoothly in **d**?
- Do your slant lines meet at the top of **A**?

Write the Alphabet

Write the missing lowercase letters.

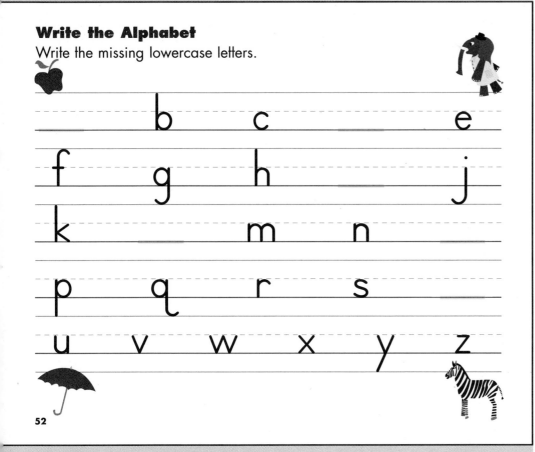

b   c   e

f   g   h   j

k   m   n

p   q   r   s

u   v   w   x   y   z

52

Write the Alphabet

Write the Alphabet pages showcase children's ability to write letters from memory. When children write a letter automatically, beginning at the correct starting point and using the correct stroke sequence, they demonstrate that they have successfully formed a clear mental and motor image of the letter.

 **Using Manipulatives**

Using manipulatives during handwriting instruction allows children to see, touch, and demonstrate the way letters are formed. Try some of the following ideas for hands-on handwriting in your classroom.

- Allow children to freely handle and experiment with their Zaner-Bloser Basic Strokes pieces.
- Form letters from clay or fun dough.
- When children are using the uppercase and lowercase alphabet cards from student pages 5–8, challenge them to arrange groups of letters that have similar shapes. Discuss similarities and differences.
- Create a center around Zaner-Bloser's interactive, write-on, wipe-off book *Now I Know My ABCs*.
- Assemble edible letters from an assortment of fruit and vegetable pieces.
- Provide Zaner-Bloser *Touch and Trace Letter Cards* for letter practice.

Apply

Sing "The Alphabet Song" with children. Ask them to clap or stand up when they hear **o, a,** or **d.** You may wish to box or highlight the letters, along with **l, i,** and **t,** on a lowercase alphabet chart you have prepared. Save the chart for use with subsequent *Write the Alphabet* pages.

Examine student page 52 with the children. Point out that there are no models on the page. Tell children they can show that they really know how to write their letters when they can write them "by heart" without any models.

Ask children to complete the page on their own, writing the missing lowercase letters within the alphabet. Observe whether children are writing these letters automatically and correctly. Celebrate their accomplishment!

Special Helps

Drawing is an important precursor to writing. Encourage children to draw regularly and to include simple geometric shapes in their drawings. Provide simple examples of how to draw everyday items, such as a cat, a two-lane road, or a flag. Children can copy and refine these simple models.

Allowing children to draw on a vertical surface, such as an easel or chalkboard, promotes shoulder strength and hand and wrist stability, which are important for handwriting success. Try this idea: Draw a picture on the chalkboard. Have children trace the lines of your picture with a paintbrush dipped in water.

—*Maureen King, O.T.R.*

Touch below the headline; **circle back** (left), ending above the baseline.

Touch below the midline; **circle back** (left), ending above the baseline.

Corrective Strategy

Place a dot for *start,* a dot for midway, and a dot for *stop* as shown. Show children how to make a backward circle stroke between the dots to form **C**.

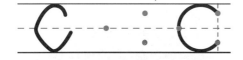

T52

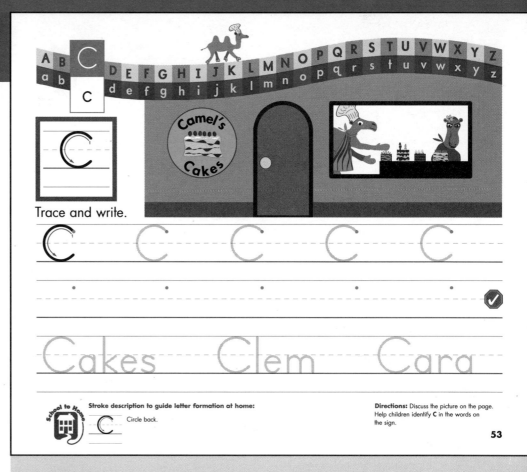

Trace and write.

Cakes   Clem   Cara

School to Home — Stroke description to guide letter formation at home: Circle back.

Directions: Discuss the picture on the page. Help children identify **C** in the words on the sign.

53

Use teaching steps 1, 2, and 3 below for pages 53 and 54 in the student book.

1. Present the Letter

Ask children to recognize the target letter in the ABC border and in the picture words. Then have them look at **C** as you discuss its shape and attributes. Talk about what basic stroke it contains and what children think it resembles. (**C** *looks like part of a circle.*)

Model Write the letter on guidelines as you say the stroke description. Have the children use their index finger to trace the model **C** in their books as you repeat the description.

Practice Let children practice writing the new letter in centers or at their tables in a variety of ways: on marker boards or slates, on large paper at an easel, in sand or finger paint.

2. Write and Evaluate

Ask children to trace the shaded letters with their finger or pencil, beginning each one at the dot. Then ask them to write a row of letters below the shaded models.

Stop and Check This icon directs children to stop and circle the best letter they wrote.

To help them evaluate **C,** ask:
- Is your **C** about the same size as the model?
- Is your **C** rounded?

To help children evaluate **c,** ask:
- Does your **c** look like a circle that has not been closed?
- Does your **c** start a little below the midline?

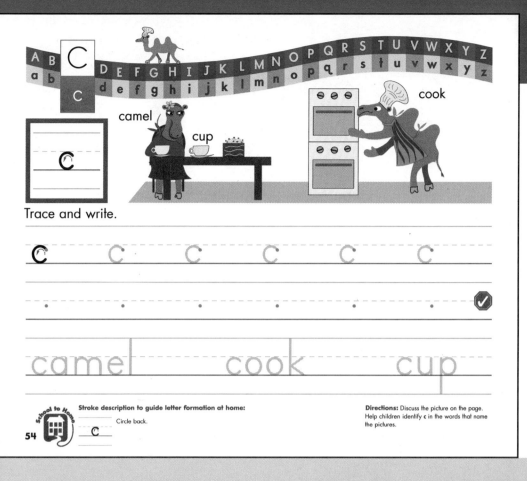

camel

cup

cook

Trace and write.

C C C C C C

camel   cook   cup

Stroke description to guide letter formation at home:

C Circle back.

Directions: Discuss the picture on the page. Help children identify **c** in the words that name the pictures.

Cc

PRACTICE MASTER 32

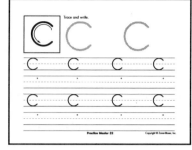

PRACTICE MASTER 33

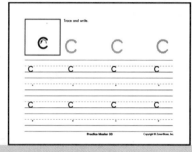

3 Apply

Ask children to trace the target letter in each shaded word with their finger or pencil. Children who are ready may trace the complete words. Relate the words to the picture at the top of the page.

School to Home

Families may use the stroke descriptions on the student page to encourage good letter formation at home. Copy and distribute **Practice Master 89** for children to take home for more practice.

Fun and Games

 auditory   visual   kinesthetic

Using Manipulatives On a bulletin board, place a column of uppercase target letters and a column of lowercase target letters in a different order. Invite children to use yarn and push pins to match the letters. (visual, kinesthetic)

Letter Hunt Take children around the classroom on a scavenger hunt for a single letter, such as **C**. Before going on this excursion, cut the letter out of magazines or write the letter several times on index cards. Hide the letters in fairly obvious places around the classroom. You might want to start the game with this chant:

We're going on a letter hunt.
We're going to find some C's
(or another letter).
Are you ready? Let's go!

Have children walk in small groups looking for the letters. You may want to repeat the chant as children search. (visual, auditory, kinesthetic)

Phonics Connection

Have each child write **Cc** on a brown paper circle (cookie). Invite children to think of words that begin with /**k**/ as in *cookie*. When a child names a word, he or she can place the cookie on a bulletin board cookie jar. (auditory, kinesthetic)

T53

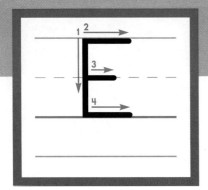

Touch the headline; **pull down straight** to the baseline. Lift. Touch the headline; **slide right**. Lift. Touch the midline; **slide right**. Stop short. Lift. Touch the baseline; **slide right**.

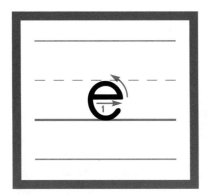

Touch halfway between the midline and baseline; **slide right; circle back** (left), ending above the baseline.

Corrective Strategy

Have children make a vertical stroke. Add three dots to show where the slide right lines should end. Point out that the middle line is shorter. Have children complete **E**.

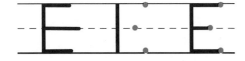

T54

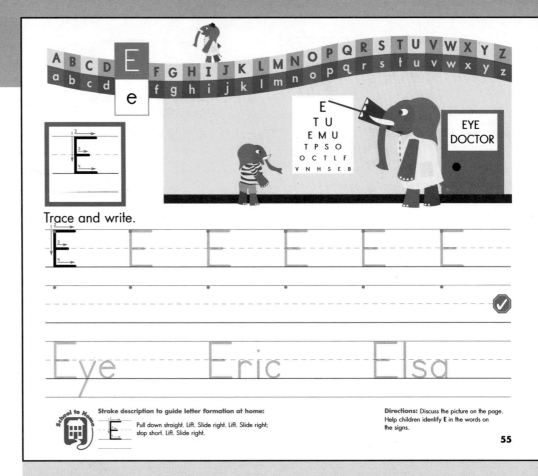

Trace and write.

Eye   Eric   Elsa

School to Home Stroke description to guide letter formation at home:
Pull down straight. Lift. Slide right. Lift. Slide right; stop short. Lift. Slide right.

Directions: Discuss the picture on the page. Help children identify **E** in the words on the signs.

55

Use teaching steps 1, 2, and 3 below for pages 55 and 56 in the student book.

1. Present the Letter

Ask children to recognize the target letter in the ABC border and in the picture words. Then direct them to look at **E**. Make sure they see that the slide right strokes are written right on the guidelines.

Model Write the letter on guidelines as you say the stroke description. Have the children use their index finger to write **E**'s on their desktop as you repeat the description and they say it with you.

Practice Let children practice writing the new letter in centers or at their tables in a variety of ways: on marker boards or slates, on large paper at an easel, in sand or finger paint.

2. Write and Evaluate

Ask children to trace the shaded letters with their finger or pencil, beginning each one at the dot. Then ask them to write a row of letters below the shaded models.

Stop and Check This icon directs children to stop and circle the best letter they wrote.

To help them evaluate **E,** ask:
• Is the vertical stroke in **E** straight?
• Are the top and bottom slide right strokes about the same?

To help children evaluate **e,** ask:
• Is your backward circle open?
• Does your **e** look round?

Trace and write.

e *e* *e* *e* *e* *e*

• • • • • • ✓

elephant   elk   ear

Stroke description to guide letter formation at home:
e   Slide right. Circle back.

Directions: Discuss the picture on the page. Help children identify **e** in the words that name the pictures.

56

School to Home

PRACTICE MASTER 34

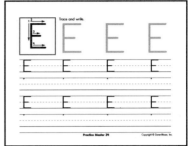

PRACTICE MASTER 35

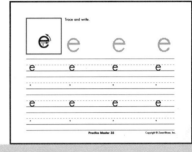

Apply

Ask children to trace the target letter in each shaded word with their finger or pencil. Children who are ready may trace the complete words. Relate the words to the picture at the top of the page.

School to Home

Families may use the stroke descriptions on the student page to encourage good letter formation at home. Copy and distribute **Practice Master 90** for children to take home for more practice.

Readiness Counts!

Size

Young children may have difficulty writing letters with correct and consistent size. Use the following activities in your classroom to develop size concepts. (See page T7 for characteristics of the pre-writer, the emergent writer, and the developing writer.)

For the Pre-Writer

Provide paper clips, buttons, wooden rods, paper squares, or other classroom items, and have the children sort them by size. As children begin to write letters, emphasize that each letter must be correctly sized to fit with the other letters in the writing.

For the Emergent Writer

Write several uppercase letters on the chalkboard. Point out that these letters are tall, just like parents are tall. Then write several short lowercase letters. Ask children to think of these letters as short—like children are short. Explain that in a roomful of people, some are short and others are tall. On a page of writing, some letters are short and others are tall.

For the Developing Writer

Children whose writing is large may require large writing spaces. Fold a sheet of unlined paper lengthwise. Three guidelines will be formed, the middle being the fold. As children become ready for a smaller writing space, provide pages from the classified ad section of the newspaper, turned on their side. The columns form guidelines for writing.

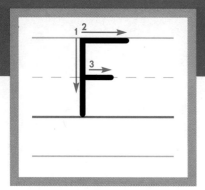

Touch the headline; **pull down straight** to the baseline. Lift. Touch the headline; **slide right**. Lift. Touch the midline; **slide right**. Stop short.

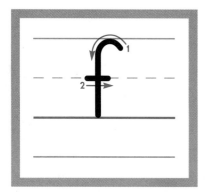

Touch below the headline; **curve back** (left); **pull down straight** to the baseline. Lift. Touch the midline; **slide right**.

Corrective Strategy

Place a green dot to show where the curve begins and another colored dot to show where the curve turns into a straight line.

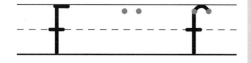

T56

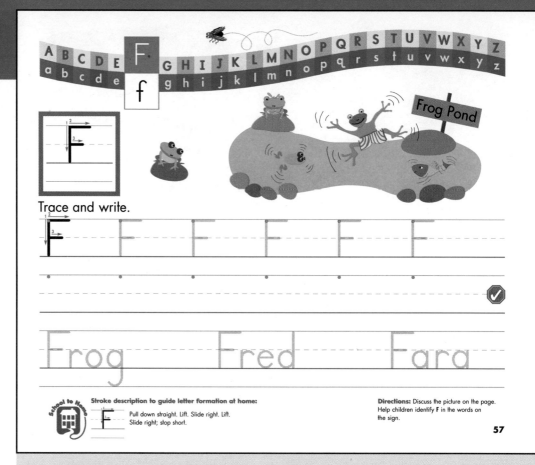

Trace and write.

F F F F F

Frog   Fred   Fara

School to Home Stroke description to guide letter formation at home:
Pull down straight. Lift. Slide right. Lift.
Slide right; stop short.

Directions: Discuss the picture on the page. Help children identify F in the words on the sign.

57

Use teaching steps 1, 2, and 3 below for pages 57 and 58 in the student book.

1. Present the Letter

Ask children to recognize the target letter in the ABC border and in the picture words. Point out that **F** is a tall letter, touching both the headline and the baseline.

Model Write the letter on guidelines as you say the stroke description. Model writing it in the air as you repeat the stroke description. Have the children say it as they write the letter in the air with you.

Practice Let children practice writing the new letter in centers or at their tables in a variety of ways: on marker boards or slates, on large paper at an easel, in sand or finger paint.

2. Write and Evaluate

Ask children to trace the shaded letters with their finger or pencil, beginning each one at the dot. Then ask them to write a row of letters below the shaded models.

 Stop and Check This icon directs children to stop and circle the best letter they wrote.

To help them evaluate **F,** ask:
- Are your strokes in **F** straight?
- Is your letter straight up and down?

To help children evaluate **f,** ask:
- Does your **f** rest on the baseline?
- Is your slide right on the midline?

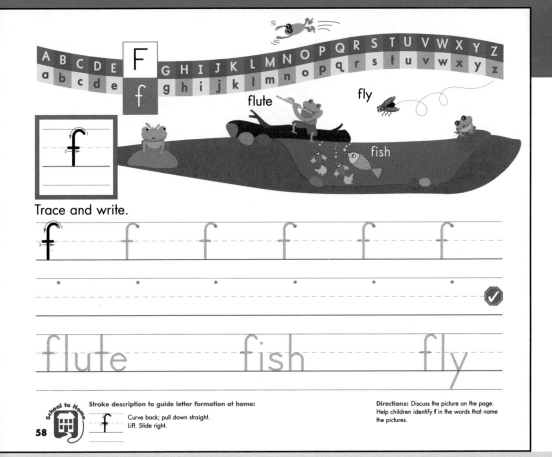

Trace and write.

f f f f f f

flute   fish   fly

Stroke description to guide letter formation at home:

f Curve back; pull down straight.
Lift. Slide right.

Directions: Discuss the picture on the page. Help children identify **f** in the words that name the pictures.

Ff

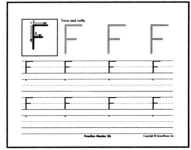
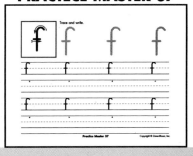
③ Apply

Ask children to trace the target letter in each shaded word with their finger or pencil. Children who are ready may trace the complete words. Relate the words to the picture at the top of the page.

School to Home

Families may use the stroke descriptions on the student page to encourage good letter formation at home. Copy and distribute **Practice Master 91** for children to take home for more practice.

Fun and Games

auditory   visual   kinesthetic

Using Manipulatives Have children use scissors to cut fish shapes out of colored construction paper. Have them write **F** and **f** on each fish. Provide paste, tape, or glue, and encourage the children to affix the fish to a bulletin board covered with blue paper. Invite them to cut bubbles and plant shapes to add to the scene. (kinesthetic)

Slide Away! Gather the children in rows facing you. Invite them to practice making slide right lines with their feet. Demonstrate how to stand with two feet together, move one foot to the right, and then the other. Play some listening music and ask the children to slide right on a given signal, perhaps at the sound of a bell or a drumbeat. You might use masking tape lines on the floor as guidelines. (auditory, visual, kinesthetic)

Phonics Connection

Explain to the children that in a tongue twister, the same sound is repeated in most words. Say this **F** tongue twister for the children. Then have them say it slowly, then quickly, with you: *Fran fed Fred's frog.* Have the children write **F** or **f** on paper. Say the tongue twister again, and have children point to **F** or **f** each time they hear /**f**/. (auditory, kinesthetic)

T57

Practice

auditory   visual   kinesthetic

Practice is critical to handwriting success. Each child benefits most from brief periods of practice done in his or her dominant learning modality. Make handwriting practice fun and engaging for children. Try these suggestions.

- Go on a "letter walk" in your classroom or school building. Look for examples of the target letter on posters, signs, and book covers. Ask children to use their fingers to trace each letter they find, following the correct stroke sequence.

- Play instrumental music as children practice writing letters. Challenge children to write along with the music.

- Provide a tub or tray of sand, salt, or other fine material. Invite children to practice writing their letters in the sand with their finger, following the correct stroke sequence.

T58

Practice

Write the letters.

c   c   e   e   f   f

C   C   E   E   F   F

59

---

1. Review the Letters

Write the letters **C, c, E, e,** and **F, f** on the chalkboard or chart paper. Invite a volunteer to come up and trace each letter you wrote as you repeat its stroke description. Next, give clues that describe one of the letters, such as *This letter looks like an upside-down j. It has one slide right stroke.* Invite children to guess the letter. (*f*) Repeat for several more letters.

2. Write and Evaluate

Remind children to check their sitting, paper, and pencil positions. Point out that there are no green starting dots on the page. Ask children if they remember where to begin each letter. Then have them complete student page 59. If time allows, challenge the children to write words that name the pictures on the page.

✓ **Stop and Check** Invite volunteers to tell how their writing has improved. To help children evaluate their letters, ask:

- Are your **c** and **C** wide open—not almost closed?
- Does the slide right stroke in your **e** touch the circle back stroke?
- Are the lines straight in **E** and **F**?
- Is the slide right stroke in your **f** near the midline?

Write the Alphabet

Write the missing uppercase letters.

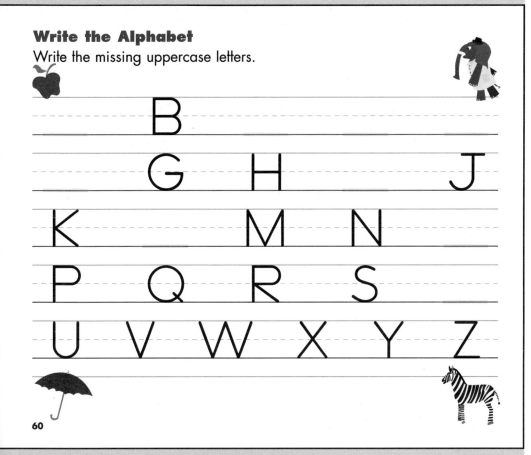

B

G   H   J

K   M   N

P   Q   R   S

U   V   W   X   Y   Z

60

Write the Alphabet

Write the Alphabet pages showcase children's ability to write letters from memory. When children write a letter automatically, beginning at the correct starting point and using the correct stroke sequence, they demonstrate that they have successfully formed a clear mental and motor image of the letter.

 **Using Manipulatives**

Using manipulatives during handwriting instruction allows children to see, touch, and demonstrate the way letters are formed. Try some of the following ideas for hands-on handwriting in your classroom.

- Assemble edible letters from an assortment of fruit and vegetable pieces.
- Provide Zaner-Bloser *Touch and Trace Letter Cards* for letter practice.
- Create a "letter town" with letter-shaped block buildings.
- Touch and trace large magnetic letters.
- Use tagboard and a hole punch to make a sewing card for each letter. Provide shoelaces for lacing.
- Challenge children to form letter shapes from rows of dry beans, buttons, counting bears, craft sticks, or other small pieces.
- Provide a variety of writing tools that interest and motivate children, including chalk, scented markers, glitter glue pens, magic slates, and sheets of newsprint.

 **Apply**

Sing "The Alphabet Song" with children. Ask them to clap or stand up when they hear **C, E,** or **F.** You may wish to add a box or highlight to these letters on the uppercase alphabet chart you prepared.

Examine student page 60 with the children. Point out that there are no models on the page that show how to write the letters. Tell children they can show that they really know how to write their letters when they can write them "by heart" without any models.

Ask children to complete the page on their own, writing the missing uppercase letters within the alphabet. Observe whether children are learning how to write these letters automatically and correctly. Celebrate their accomplishment!

Special Helps

The chalkboard is an important tool for handwriting instruction. Children enjoy writing at the board, and the amount of sensory feedback created between chalk and board is an advantage for developing essential fine motor and perceptual skills.

It is important to realize that chalkboards and dry-erase boards do not serve the same functions when it comes to handwriting instruction. For many children, dry-erase markers flow too quickly to aid careful formation of letters. The fluidity of markers can be useful, however, for children who apply too much pencil pressure when writing.

—Maureen King, O.T.R.

Touch below the headline; **circle back** (left), ending at the midline. **Slide left**.

Touch below the midline; **circle back** (left) all the way around. **Push up straight** to the midline. **Pull down straight** through the baseline; **curve back** (left).

Alternate Letter Formation

Use this stroke description to show an alternate method for children who have difficulty using the continuous-stroke method.

 Circle back all the way around. **Lift.** **Pull down straight; curve back**.

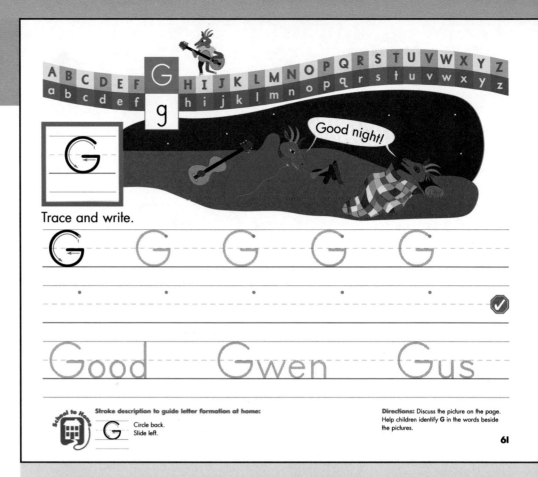

Trace and write.

G   G   G   G   G

Good   Gwen   Gus

Stroke description to guide letter formation at home:

G   Circle back.
    Slide left.

Directions: Discuss the picture on the page. Help children identify **G** in the words beside the pictures.

61

Use teaching steps 1, 2, and 3 below for pages 61 and 62 in the student book.

1. Present the Letter

Ask children to recognize the target letter in the ABC border and in the picture words. Focus on the shape of **G** by having the children describe what it looks like. (*a circle with one piece broken in; a C with an extra line*)

Model Write the letter on guidelines as you say the stroke description. Invite volunteers to dip a large paintbrush in water and write **G** on the chalkboard as they repeat the stroke description with you.

Practice Let children practice writing the new letter in centers or at their tables in a variety of ways: on marker boards or slates, on large paper at an easel, in sand or finger paint.

2. Write and Evaluate

Ask children to trace the shaded letters with their finger or pencil, beginning each one at the dot. Then ask them to write a row of letters below the shaded models.

✔ **Stop and Check** This icon directs children to stop and circle the best letter they wrote.

To help them evaluate **G,** ask:
• Is your **G** about the same size as the model?
• Is your slide left on the midline?

To help children evaluate **g,** ask:
• Is your **g** made with a backward circle stroke?
• Does your **g** end below the baseline?

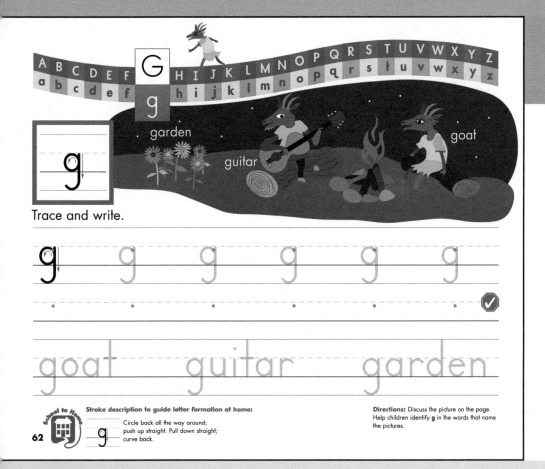

Trace and write.

g g g g g g g

goat guitar garden

School to Home
Stroke description to guide letter formation at home:

g Circle back all the way around;
push up straight. Pull down straight;
curve back.

62

Directions: Discuss the picture on the page.
Help children identify **g** in the words that name
the pictures.

PRACTICE MASTER 38

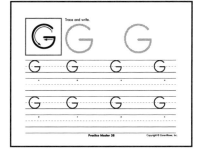

PRACTICE MASTER 39

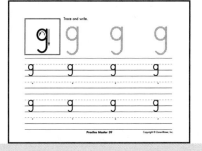

---

3 Apply

Ask children to trace the target
letter in each shaded word with
their finger or pencil. Children
who are ready may trace the
complete words. Relate the words
to the picture at the top of the
page.

School to Home

Families may use the stroke
descriptions on the student
page to encourage good letter
formation at home. Copy and
distribute **Practice Master 92**
for children to take home for
more practice.

Readiness Counts!

Guidelines

Children vary in their ability to
write within the confines of a des-
ignated area. It is your responsibility to decide what type of paper is
best for the children in your class.
(See page T7 for characteristics of
the pre-writer, the emergent writer,
and the developing writer.)

For the Pre-Writer
By folding a sheet of unlined
paper, you can create writing
spaces of the size that is best for
individual children. At first, fold
the paper only once the long way
(horizontal). You now have a headline (the top of the paper), a midline (the fold of the paper), and a
baseline (the bottom of the paper).

When the children are ready for
smaller writing spaces, just fold
the paper again and you will have
a headline, midline, baseline, and
descender space.

For the Emergent Writer
The classified ad section of the
newspaper serves well as writing
paper for young children. Place the
paper on the desk so the columns
run horizontally to provide writing
spaces.

For the Developing Writer
Help the children practice using
the term "halfway" and locating
the halfway point between two
lines. Make two horizontal parallel
lines with masking tape on the
floor. Have the children take turns
taking one jump to the halfway
point between the lines. Ask each
child to decide whether the
halfway point was reached. If not,
ask his or her classmates to help
guide the child to the correct spot.

Touch the headline; **pull down straight; curve back** (left). Lift. Touch the headline; **slide right**.

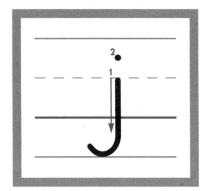

Touch the midline; **pull down straight** through the baseline; **curve back** (left). Lift. **Dot.**

Corrective Strategy

Make several vertical lines ending above the baseline. Add two dots, as shown. Then have children write the curve.

T62

Trace and write.

J J J J J

Jack   Jill   Jug

School to Home — **Stroke description to guide letter formation at home:**
J   Pull down straight; curve back. Lift. Slide right.

Directions: Discuss the picture on the page. Help children identify J in the picture.

63

Use teaching steps 1, 2, and 3 below for pages 63 and 64 in the student book.

1. Present the Letter

Ask children to recognize the target letter in the ABC border and in the picture words. Write **J** on guidelines as you say the stroke description. Make sure children notice that the slide right stroke is on the headline.

Model Write the letter on guidelines as you say the stroke description. Model writing it in the air as you repeat the stroke description. Have the children say it with you as they trace **J** in the model box on the student page.

Practice Let children practice writing the new letter in centers or at their tables in a variety of ways: on marker boards or slates, on large paper at an easel, in sand or finger paint.

2. Write and Evaluate

Ask children to trace the shaded letters with their finger or pencil, beginning each one at the dot. Then ask them to write a row of letters below the shaded models.

✔ **Stop and Check** This icon directs children to stop and circle the best letter they wrote.

To help them evaluate **J,** ask:
• Does your **J** begin near the headline?
• Is your slide right on the headline?

To help children evaluate **j,** ask:
• Does your **j** begin near the midline?
• Is the bottom of your **j** round?

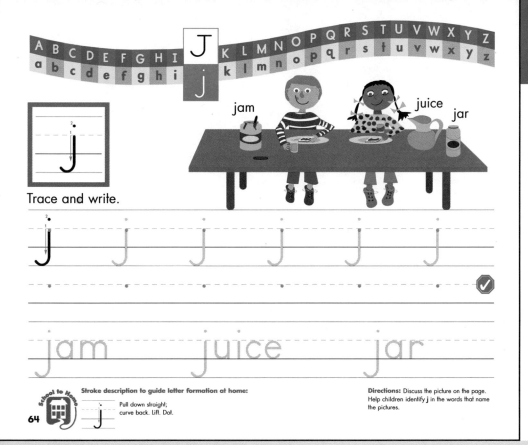

Trace and write.

jam   juice   jar

jam   juice   jar

Stroke description to guide letter formation at home:

j   Pull down straight; curve back. Lift. Dot.

Directions: Discuss the picture on the page. Help children identify **j** in the words that name the pictures.

PRACTICE MASTER 40

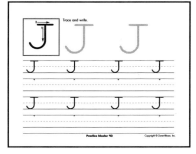

PRACTICE MASTER 41

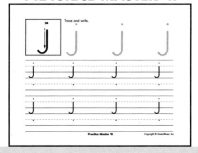

Apply

Ask children to trace the target letter in each shaded word with their finger or pencil. Children who are ready may trace the complete words. Relate the words to the picture at the top of the page.

Families may use the stroke descriptions on the student page to encourage good letter formation at home. Copy and distribute **Practice Master 93** for children to take home for more practice.

Fun and Games

 auditory   visual   kinesthetic

Using Manipulatives
Invite children to make the letters **J** and **j** from modeling clay. Encourage them to roll a ball of clay between the palms of their hands to make a rope and then shape the rope into a letter. Remind them to add the slide right to **J** and the dot to **j**. (kinesthetic, visual, auditory)

Musical Alphabet Give
each child a card with a letter printed on it. Have children hold the cards on their laps as they sing this adaptation of a popular song:

*If you have a **J** in your lap, give a clap.*
*If you have a **J** in your lap, give a clap.*
*If you have a **J** in your lap, don't be shy, give a clap.*
*If you have a **J** in your lap, give a clap!*

You may wish to have children make different motions for each letter as they sing. (visual, auditory, kinesthetic)

Phonics Connection

Write guidelines on the chalkboard. After everyone agrees that *jam* begins with /**j**/, ask the children to jump up every time they hear a word that begins like *jam*. Say other words, some that begin with **j**. Have a child write **j** on the chalkboard if the word begins with **j**. (auditory, kinesthetic)

T63

Touch below the headline; **circle back** (left) all the way around. **Slant right** to the baseline.

Touch below the midline; **circle back** (left) all the way around. **Push up straight** to the midline. **Pull down straight** through the baseline; **curve forward** (right).

Alternate Letter Formation

Use this stroke description to show an alternate method for children who have difficulty using the continuous-stroke method.

 Circle back all the way around. **Lift. Pull down straight; curve forward**.

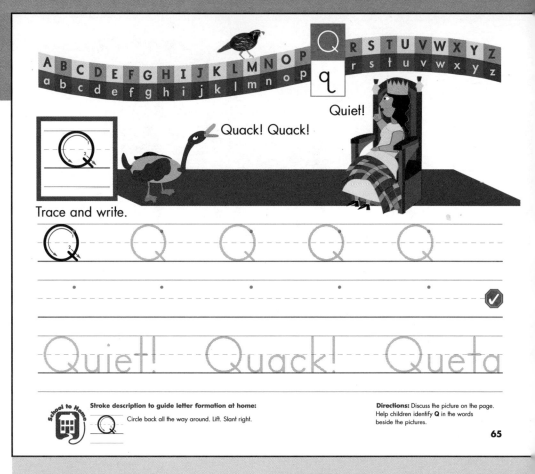

Trace and write.

Quiet!

Quack! Quack!

Quiet! Quack! Queta

School to Home Stroke description to guide letter formation at home:

Q̲ Circle back all the way around. Lift. Slant right.

Directions: Discuss the picture on the page. Help children identify **Q** in the words beside the pictures.

65

Use teaching steps 1, 2, and 3 below for pages 65 and 66 in the student book.

1 Present the Letter

Ask children to recognize the target letter in the ABC border and in the picture words. Help children find the card for **Q** in their Uppercase Alphabet Cards. (See pages T4 and T5.) Ask what other letter they see in **Q**. (*O*)

Model Write the letter on guidelines as you say the stroke description. Model writing it in the air as you repeat the stroke description. Have the children say it as they write the letter in the air with you.

Practice Let children practice writing the new letter in centers or at their tables in a variety of ways: on marker boards or slates, on large paper at an easel, in sand or finger paint.

2 Write and Evaluate

Ask children to trace the shaded letters with their finger or pencil, beginning each one at the dot. Then ask them to write a row of letters below the shaded models.

✓ **Stop and Check** This icon directs children to stop and circle the best letter they wrote.

To help them evaluate **Q**, ask:
• Does your **Q** look like **O** except for the slant right stroke?
• Does your slant right end near the baseline?

To help children evaluate **q**, ask:
• Is your **q** made with a backward circle stroke?
• Does your **q** go below the baseline?

T64

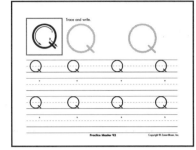

Qq

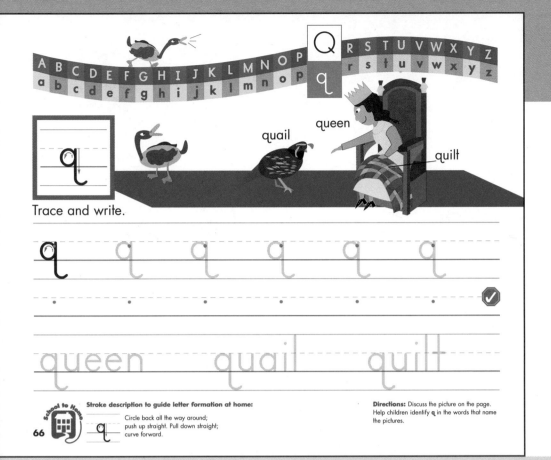

Trace and write.

queen

quail

queen

quail

quilt

 Stroke description to guide letter formation at home:

Circle back all the way around; push up straight. Pull down straight; curve forward.

Directions: Discuss the picture on the page. Help children identify **q** in the words that name the pictures.

PRACTICE MASTER 42

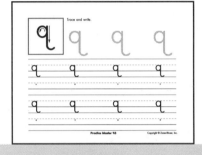

PRACTICE MASTER 43

Apply

Ask children to trace the target letter in each shaded word with their finger or pencil. Children who are ready may trace the complete words. Relate the words to the picture at the top of the page.

School to Home

Families may use the stroke descriptions on the student page to encourage good letter formation at home. Copy and distribute **Practice Master 94** for children to take home for more practice.

Readiness Counts!

Reversals

Young children with directionality problems (moving from left to right across the page) may tend to reverse basic strokes when writing. This interferes with the ability to form letters correctly. Use the following activities in your classroom to improve reversal problems. (See page T7 for characteristics of the pre-writer, the emergent writer, and the developing writer.)

For the Pre-Writer

Provide opportunities for the child to write at the chalkboard within a confined area with frequent arrows as a reminder of left-to-right progression. In addition, prepare sheets of paper on which the left edges and the beginning stroke of a letter, such as **q,** are colored green.

For the Emergent Writer

Emphasize each step of the stroke description before the child writes a letter. Provide a letter for tracing that has been colored according to stroke order. Repeat the stroke description with the child as he or she writes the letter.

For the Developing Writer

Provide pipe cleaners or ropes of clay for children to make circles and vertical strokes. Help them recognize that they should place the circle first for **a, d, g,** and **q.** The vertical stroke comes after the circle in these letters. For **b** and **p,** however, the vertical stroke comes first.

Practice

Practice

auditory visual kinesthetic

Practice is critical to handwriting success. Each child benefits most from brief periods of practice done in his or her dominant learning modality. Practice activities that provide meaningful purposes for writing are best. Try these suggestions.

- Choose two target letters. Ask pairs of children to use these in place of **X**'s and **O**'s as they play Tic-Tac-Toe.

- Have one partner describe the correct stroke sequence for the target letter as the other partner writes it several times. Then switch roles.

- Form a large letter on the classroom floor with masking tape. Invite children to walk, skip, or hop along the letter several times, following the correct stroke sequence.

T66

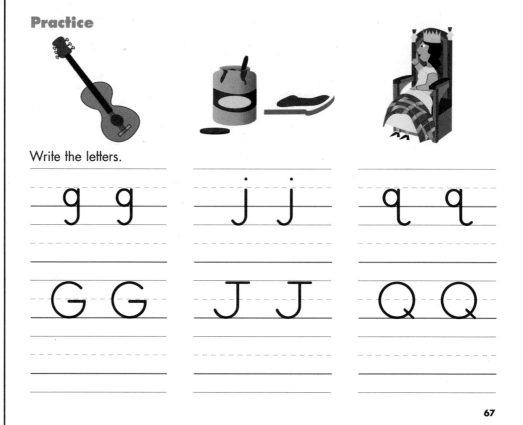

Write the letters.

g g   j j   q q

G G   J J   Q Q

67

1. Review the Letters

Write the letters **G, g, J, j,** and **Q, q** on the chalkboard or chart paper. Invite a volunteer to come up and trace each letter you wrote as you repeat its stroke description. Next, give clues that describe one of the letters, such as *This letter has a tall circle. It looks like a lollipop on a short stick.* Invite children to guess the letter. (*Q*) Repeat for several more letters.

2. Write and Evaluate

Remind children to check their sitting, paper, and pencil positions. Point out that there are no green starting dots on the page. Ask children if they remember where to begin each letter. Then have them complete student page 67. If time allows, challenge the children to write words that name the pictures on the page.

✓ **Stop and Check** Praise children's progress in writing these letters. Invite volunteers to tell how their writing has improved. To help children evaluate their letters, ask:

- Did you write the "tails" correctly on **g** and **q**?
- Does your **G** have a good slide left stroke?
- Did you dot your **j**?
- Does your **J** have its "hat" on?

Write the Alphabet
Write the missing lowercase letters.

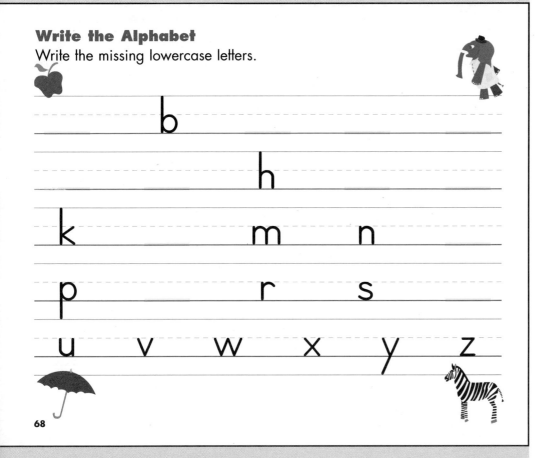

b

h

k   m   n

p   r   s

u   v   w   x   y   z

68

Write the Alphabet pages showcase children's ability to write letters from memory. When children write a letter automatically, beginning at the correct starting point and using the correct stroke sequence, they demonstrate that they have successfully formed a clear mental and motor image of the letter.

 ## Using Manipulatives

Using manipulatives during handwriting instruction allows children to see, touch, and demonstrate the way letters are formed. Try some of the following ideas for hands-on handwriting in your classroom.

- Allow children to freely handle and experiment with their Zaner-Bloser Basic Strokes pieces.
- Form letters from clay or fun dough.
- When children are using the uppercase and lowercase alphabet cards from student pages 5–8, challenge them to arrange groups of letters that have similar shapes. Discuss similarities and differences.
- Create a center around Zaner-Bloser's interactive, write-on, wipe-off book *Now I Know My ABCs.*
- Assemble edible letters from an assortment of fruit and vegetable pieces.
- Provide Zaner-Bloser *Touch and Trace Letter Cards* for letter practice.
- Create a "letter town" with letter-shaped block buildings.
- Touch and trace large magnetic letters.

3 Apply

Sing "The Alphabet Song" with children. Ask them to clap or stand up when they hear **g, j,** or **q**. You may wish to add a box or highlight to these letters on the lowercase alphabet chart you prepared.

Examine student page 68 with the children. Point out that there are no models on the page that show how to write the letters. Tell children they can show that they really know how to write their letters when they can write them "by heart" without any models.

Ask children to complete the page on their own, writing the missing lowercase letters within the alphabet. Observe whether children are learning how to write these letters automatically and correctly. Celebrate their accomplishment!

Special Helps

Handwriting is a complex task that requires mental focus and physical control. Take advantage of "slow down" times during the day and involve children in fine motor activities that help concentration and finger control.

Allow children to play tower-building and balancing games such as Jenga for help with controlled release and placement of objects. Duplicate a practice sheet of checker-sized circles. Anchor checkers to a tabletop with masking tape to increase their resistance to being picked up. Challenge children to pick up the checkers with their fingertips and align them inside the circles.

—*Maureen King, O.T.R.*

T67

Touch the headline; **pull down straight; curve forward** (right); **push up** to the headline.

Touch the midline; **pull down straight; curve forward** (right); **push up** to the midline. **Pull down straight** to the baseline.

Corrective Strategy

Draw a dotted line across **U** to show where the curve forward stroke begins and ends. Have children trace the letter.

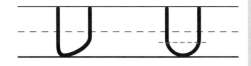

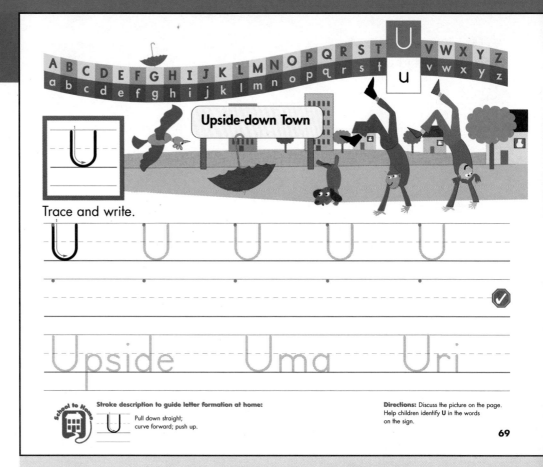

Upside-down Town

Trace and write.

Upside   Uma   Uri

School to Home Stroke description to guide letter formation at home:
Pull down straight; curve forward; push up.

Directions: Discuss the picture on the page. Help children identify **U** in the words on the sign.

69

Use teaching steps 1, 2, and 3 below for pages 69 and 70 in the student book.

1. Present the Letter

Ask children to recognize the target letter in the ABC border and in the picture words. Help them notice that **U** has two pull down straight strokes connected to part of a circle at the bottom.

Model Write the letter on guidelines as you say the stroke description. Model writing it in the air as you repeat the stroke description. Have the children say it as they use their index finger to write the letter on their desktop.

Practice Let children practice writing the new letter in centers or at their tables in a variety of ways: on marker boards or slates, on large paper at an easel, in sand or finger paint.

2. Write and Evaluate

Ask children to trace the shaded letters with their finger or pencil, beginning each one at the dot. Then ask them to write a row of letters below the shaded models.

Stop and Check This icon directs children to stop and circle the best letter they wrote.

To help them evaluate **U,** ask:
• Does your **U** begin at the headline?
• Is the curve of your **U** round?

To help children evaluate **u,** ask:
• Does the curve of your **u** rest on the baseline?
• Are your vertical strokes straight?

umbrella

up

under

Trace and write.

U

umbrella   up   under

Directions: Discuss the picture on the page. Help children identify **u** in the words that name the pictures.

PRACTICE MASTER 44

Trace and write.

U U U U

PRACTICE MASTER 45

Trace and write.

u u u

---

③ Apply

Ask children to trace the target letter in each shaded word with their finger or pencil. Children who are ready may trace the complete words. Relate the words to the picture at the top of the page.

Families may use the stroke descriptions on the student page to encourage good letter formation at home. Copy and distribute **Practice Master 95** for children to take home for more practice.

Fun and Games

auditory   visual   kinesthetic

Using Manipulatives To promote fine-motor control, provide short lengths of yarn and pictures of shoes. Have children glue the yarn to the shoe to show shoelaces that are untied. When the glue is dry, encourage children to tie the yarn into a bow. Alternatively, provide actual shoes and encourage the children to demonstrate their lace-tying skills. (kinesthetic)

Getaway Draw a mouse on one end of the chalkboard. Make a trail of letters across the chalkboard leading to a "mouse hole."

Write several **u**'s on the trail so each child can trace one. Ask the children to help the mouse escape from the cat and reach its hole by tracing the **u**'s on the trail with colored chalk. (visual, kinesthetic)

Phonics Connection

Write the word *up* on the chalkboard or on large chart paper and read it for the children. Tell the children that the letter **u** begins the word *up*. Pronounce the short **u** sound (**/uh/**). Say words such as these, and have the children repeat each one with you: *up, underground, dog, umpire, upside-down, lizard, umbrella, under, house, playground, ugly, until, up-and-down, paper, usher.* Have children raise their hand only if they hear a word that begins like *up*. (auditory)

Touch below the headline;
curve back (left); **curve forward** (right), ending above the baseline.

Touch below the midline;
curve back (left); **curve forward** (right), ending above the baseline.

Corrective Strategy

Draw one circle above another circle as shown and outline the backward and forward curves of **S** that form part of a circle.

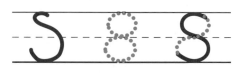

T70

Trace and write.

S S S S S

Stop School Street

School to Home

S   Curve back;
    curve forward.

Stroke description to guide letter formation at home:

Directions: Discuss the picture on the page. Help children identify **S** in the words on the signs.

71

Use teaching steps 1, 2, and 3 below for pages 71 and 72 in the student book.

1. Present the Letter

Ask children to recognize the target letter in the ABC border and in the picture words. Then have them look at **S** as you talk about what basic strokes it contains. Ask if the children can see parts of both forward and backward circles in the letter.

Model Write the letter on guidelines as you say the stroke description. Model writing it in the air as you repeat the stroke description. Have the children form backward and forward circles in the air as they say the stroke description with you.

Practice Let children practice writing the new letter in centers or at their tables in a variety of ways: on marker boards or slates, on large paper at an easel, in sand or finger paint.

2. Write and Evaluate

Ask children to trace the shaded letters with their finger or pencil, beginning each one at the dot. Then ask them to write a row of letters below the shaded models.

Stop and Check This icon directs children to stop and circle the best letter they wrote.

To help them evaluate **S,** ask:
- Is your **S** about the same size as the model?
- Are the top and bottom of your **S** about the same size?

To help children evaluate **s,** ask:
- Are the curved parts of your **s** round?
- Is the top part of your **s** about the same size as the bottom part?

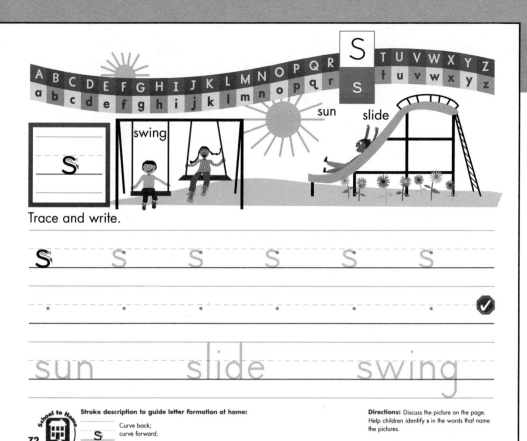

Trace and write.

S   s   s   s   s   s   s   s

sun   slide   swing

Ss

PRACTICE MASTER 46

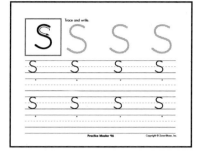

PRACTICE MASTER 47

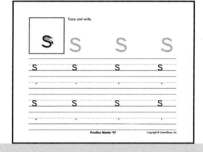

Apply

Ask children to trace the target letter in each shaded word with their finger or pencil. Children who are ready may trace the complete words. Relate the words to the picture at the top of the page.

School to Home

Families may use the stroke descriptions on the student page to encourage good letter formation at home. Copy and distribute **Practice Master 96** for children to take home for more practice.

Readiness Counts!

Fine Motor Skills

When a child demonstrates problems in performing a fine-motor action, such as handwriting or using scissors, the teacher can provide activities that promote motor development. Use the following activities in your classroom to develop fine-motor skills. (See page T7 for characteristics of the pre-writer, the emergent writer, and the developing writer.)

For the Pre-Writer
If a child tends to break or crush small objects in the hand without meaning to, provide an eyedropper and have him or her use it to release one drop of colored water at a time to decorate a design on a paper towel or a clean coffee filter.

For the Emergent Writer
Tape one end of a strip of paper with a line drawn down the middle to the edge of a table or desk. Have the child sit on the floor, holding the dangling end of the paper strip in his or her nonpreferred hand. Make sure the child holds the scissors correctly, and tell him or her to cut upward along the line. This will strengthen the elbow and foster the child's ability to write with greater precision.

For the Developing Writer
For a child who fails to use the "other" hand to steady the paper when writing, provide about 15–20 round, flat objects and instruct him or her to stack them, one at a time, on a flat surface—with eyes closed. The nonpreferred hand provides sensory feedback in order to accomplish the task.

Touch the headline; **pull down straight** to the baseline. Lift. Touch the headline; **slide right; curve forward** (right) to the midline; **slide left. Slide right; curve forward** (right) to the baseline. **Slide left**.

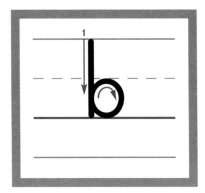

Touch the headline; **pull down straight** to the baseline. **Push up; circle forward** (right) all the way around.

Corrective Strategy

Place dots to show children where to begin and end the vertical stroke and how to write the push up stroke and the forward circle.

T72

Trace and write.

Baby Bear   Bert

School to Home

Stroke description to guide letter formation at home:

B Pull down straight. Lift. Slide right; curve forward; slide left. Slide right; curve forward; slide left.

Directions: Discuss the picture on the page. Help children identify **B** in the words on the sign.

73

Use teaching steps 1, 2, and 3 below for pages 73 and 74 in the student book.

1. Present the Letter

Ask children to recognize the target letter in the ABC border and in the picture words. Have children look at **B** and notice how it fits between the headline and the baseline. Then talk about what basic strokes the letter contains.

Model Write the letter on guidelines as you say the stroke description. Have the children trace the model **B** in their books as you repeat the description.

Practice Let children practice writing the new letter in centers or at their tables in a variety of ways: on marker boards or slates, on large paper at an easel, in sand or finger paint.

2. Write and Evaluate

Ask children to trace the shaded letters with their finger or pencil, beginning each one at the dot. Then ask them to write a row of letters below the shaded models.

Stop and Check This icon directs children to stop and circle the best letter they wrote.

To help them evaluate **B,** ask:
- Is your **B** about the same size as the model?
- Are the curves of your **B** round?

To help children evaluate **b,** ask:
- Is your **b** straight up and down?
- Is your forward circle round?

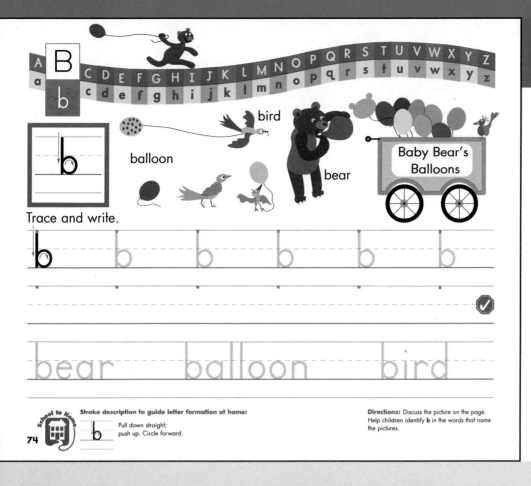

Trace and write.

b b b b b

bear balloon bird

Directions: Discuss the picture on the page. Help children identify **b** in the words that name the pictures.

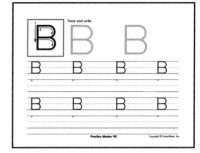
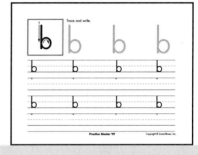
3 Apply

Ask children to trace the target letter in each shaded word with their finger or pencil. Children who are ready may trace the complete words. Relate the words to the picture at the top of the page.

School to Home

Families may use the stroke descriptions on the student page to encourage good letter formation at home. Copy and distribute **Practice Master 97** for children to take home for more practice.

Fun and Games

 auditory   visual   kinesthetic

Using Manipulatives

Provide dried beans for children to glue to a piece of paper to make a "Bean Page." Encourage them to use glue to write the letter and then to attach the beans one by one to fill out the letter's shape. (kinesthetic, visual)

Grocery Store Print letters on the outside of brown paper bags. Write single letters on the outside of empty food containers. Encourage children to sort the groceries into their matching letter bags. This game is fun in the dramatic play area. (visual, kinesthetic)

Phonics Connection

Write the word *cat* on the chalkboard and read it with the children. Then ask someone to erase **c** and write **b** in its place. Have the children read the new word with you. Repeat the activity with the following word pairs, each time writing **b**.

park to *bark, top* to *bop, mat* to *bat, call* to *ball, sent* to *bent, fare* to *bare*

(visual, auditory, kinesthetic)

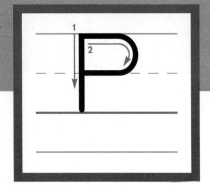

Touch the headline; **pull down straight** to the baseline. Lift. Touch the headline; **slide right; curve forward** (right) to the midline; **slide left**.

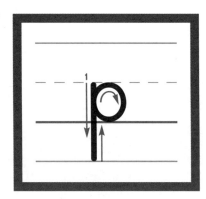

Touch the midline; **pull down straight** through the baseline to the next guideline. **Push up; curve forward** (right) all the way around.

Corrective Strategy

Place dots to indicate where the slide right ends and where the slide left begins. Show how the curve is made between the two dots.

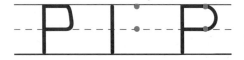

T74

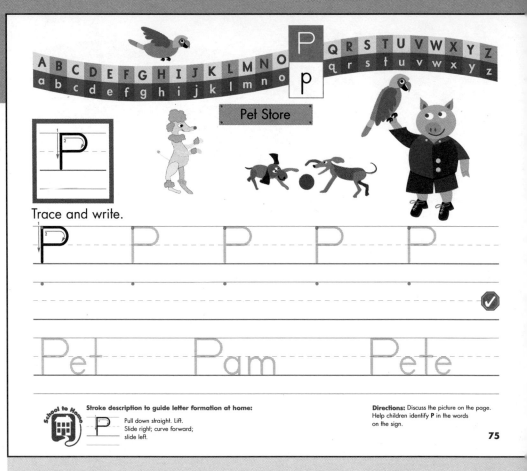

Pet Store

Trace and write.

P

Pet   Pam   Pete

School to Home

Stroke description to guide letter formation at home:

P Pull down straight. Lift.
Slide right; curve forward;
slide left.

Directions: Discuss the picture on the page. Help children identify **P** in the words on the sign.

75

Use teaching steps 1, 2, and 3 below for pages 75 and 76 in the student book.

1. Present the Letter

Ask children to recognize the target letter in the ABC border and in the picture words. Then have them look at **P** as you discuss its shape and attributes. Talk about what basic strokes it contains. (*pull down straight, slide right, curve forward, slide left*)

Model Write the letter on guidelines as you say the stroke description. Model writing it in the air as you repeat the stroke description. Have the children say it as they write the letter in the air with you.

Practice Let children practice writing the new letter in centers or at their tables in a variety of ways: on marker boards or slates, on large paper at an easel, in sand or finger paint.

2. Write and Evaluate

Ask children to trace the shaded letters with their finger or pencil, beginning each one at the dot. Then ask them to write a row of letters below the shaded models.

 Stop and Check This icon directs children to stop and circle the best letter they wrote.

To help them evaluate **P,** ask:
- Is your **P** straight up and down?
- Is your **P** about the same size as the model?

To help children evaluate **p,** ask:
- Is your **p** straight up and down?
- Is your forward circle round?

Pp

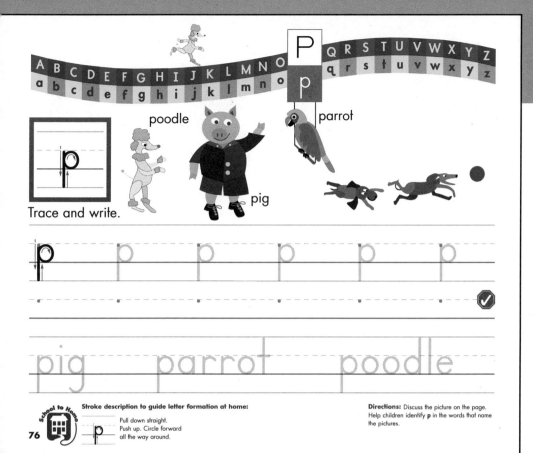

poodle

parrot

pig

Trace and write.

p p p p p p

pig   parrot   poodle

Directions: Discuss the picture on the page.
Help children identify **p** in the words that name
the pictures.

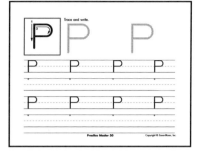
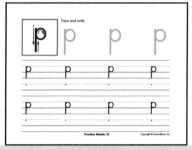
Apply

Ask children to trace the target
letter in each shaded word with
their finger or pencil. Children
who are ready may trace the
complete words. Relate the words
to the picture at the top of the
page.

School to Home

Families may use the stroke
descriptions on the student
page to encourage good letter
formation at home. Copy and
distribute **Practice Master 98**
for children to take home for
more practice.

Readiness Counts!

Reversals

Young children frequently reverse
letters with similar shapes, such as
b and **d** and **g** and **q**. Reversals
will diminish as children internal-
ize left-to-right writing and the
unique formation of each letter.
(See page T7 for characteristics of
the pre-writer, the emergent writer,
and the developing writer.)

For the Pre-Writer

Use words such as **left, right, in
front of, before,** and **after** as you
play gross-motor games. Discuss
frequently confused letters such as
g and **q** by making comments such
as "**g** says 'good-night' and curls
its tail under. **q** is quick; its tail
flies out behind."

For the Emergent Writer

Teach frequently reversed letters
on different days. Encourage children to use clay, pipe cleaners,
Basic Strokes pieces, and other
materials to model each letter.
Then ask them to close their eyes
briefly and form a clear mental
image of the letter before writing.

For the Developing Writer

Challenge children to write frequently confused letters correctly
as you say the stroke descriptions.
Check to see that children are
beginning to write automatically,
without stopping to think too much
about letter formation.

Practice

auditory   visual   kinesthetic

Practice is critical to handwriting success. Each child benefits most from brief periods of practice done in his or her dominant learning modality. Too much practice of letters in isolation is frustrating for most children and promotes sloppy writing. Instead, try these suggestions.

- Teach children a "Look, Write, Check" strategy. Children first look at the target letter model in their books for a few seconds to form a clear mental image of the letter. Next, they cover the model with their hands and write the letter 3–4 times. Last, they uncover the model and compare it to the letters they wrote.

- Make an audiotape of yourself saying the stroke descriptions found in this book for a group of target letters. Ask children to listen to the tape with headphones in the writing center as they practice their letters.

- Dispense a small amount of shaving cream onto each desk or tabletop. Invite children to use their fingers to write target letters 3–4 times in the shaving cream. Remind children to begin their letters at the correct starting point and to use the correct stroke sequence. Then wipe the surfaces clean.

Practice

Write the letters.

u u   s s   b b   p p

U   S   B   P

---

1 Review the Letters

Write the letters **U, u, S, s, B, b,** and **P, p** on the chalkboard or chart paper. Invite a volunteer to come up and trace each letter you wrote as you repeat its stroke description. Next, give clues that describe one of the letters, such as *This letter looks like uppercase B without the lower "bump." It is tall.* Invite children to guess the letter. (**P**) Repeat for several more letters.

2 Write and Evaluate

Remind children to check their sitting, paper, and pencil positions. Point out that there are no green starting dots on the page. Ask children if they remember where to begin each letter. Then have them complete student page 77. If time allows, challenge the children to write words that name the pictures on the page.

✓ **Stop and Check** Praise children's progress in writing these letters. Invite volunteers to tell how their writing has improved. To help children evaluate their letters, ask:

- Is your **U** not too skinny or too fat—about the same width as the model?
- Do your **S** and **s** look the same except for size?
- Did you begin **b** at the top?
- Did you retrace smoothly on **p**?

Write the Alphabet
Write the missing uppercase letters.

H

K M N

R

V W X Y Z

78

Write the Alphabet pages showcase children's ability to write letters from memory. When children write a letter automatically, beginning at the correct starting point and using the correct stroke sequence, they demonstrate that they have successfully formed a clear mental and motor image of the letter.

Using Manipulatives

Using manipulatives during handwriting instruction allows children to see, touch, and demonstrate the way that letters are formed. Try some of the following ideas for hands-on handwriting in your classroom.

- Create a center around Zaner-Bloser's interactive, write-on, wipe-off book *Now I Know My ABCs.*
- Assemble edible letters from an assortment of fruit and vegetable pieces.
- Provide Zaner-Bloser *Touch and Trace Letter Cards* for letter practice.
- Create a "letter town" with letter-shaped block buildings.
- Touch and trace large magnetic letters.
- Use tagboard and a hole punch to make a sewing card for each letter. Provide shoelaces for lacing.
- Challenge children to form letter shapes from rows of dry beans, buttons, counting bears, craft sticks, or other small pieces.
- Provide a variety of writing tools that interest and motivate children, including chalk, scented markers, glitter glue pens, magic slates, and sheets of newsprint.

3 Apply

Sing "The Alphabet Song" with children. Ask them to clap or stand up when they hear **U, S, B,** or **P.** You may wish to add a box or highlight to these letters on the uppercase alphabet chart you prepared.

Examine student page 78 with the children. Point out that there are no models on the page that show how to write the letters. Tell children they can show that they really know how to write their letters when they can write them "by heart" without any models.

Ask children to complete the page on their own, writing the missing uppercase letters within the alphabet. Observe whether children are learning how to write these letters automatically and correctly. Celebrate their accomplishment!

Special Helps

Learning to distinguish between letterforms with similar shapes, such as **b** and **d, p** and **q, m** and **n,** and **n** and **u,** is an important perceptual skill. Make flashcards of these frequently confused letters and use them to assess children's ability to distinguish the letters. For further practice, prepare bingo cards that show the tricky letters along with other letters and numerals. Have children use their fingertips to place buttons, beans, or small scraps of paper over one example of the letters you call out.

—*Maureen King, O.T.R.*

Touch the headline; **pull down straight** to the baseline. Lift. Touch the headline; **slide right; curve forward** (right) to the midline; **slide left. Slant right** to the baseline.

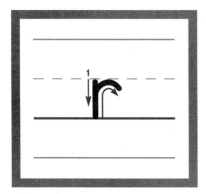

Touch the midline; **pull down straight** to the baseline. **Push up; curve forward** (right).

Corrective Strategy

To help children avoid writing **r** with a loop, have them carefully retrace the vertical stroke. To show where to start and finish the curve forward stroke of **r,** add dots and have children complete the letter.

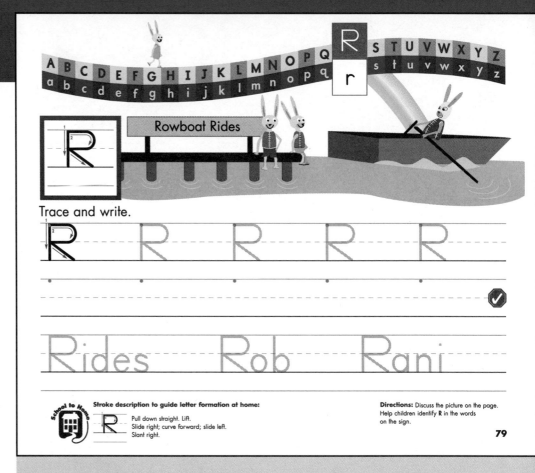

Rowboat Rides

Trace and write.

R R R R R

Rides   Rob   Rani

School to Home **Stroke description to guide letter formation at home:**

R Pull down straight. Lift.
Slide right; curve forward; slide left.
Slant right.

Directions: Discuss the picture on the page. Help children identify **R** in the words on the sign.

79

Use teaching steps 1, 2, and 3 below for pages 79 and 80 in the student book.

1. Present the Letter

Ask children to recognize the target letter in the ABC border and in the picture words. Then have them look at **R** as you discuss its shape and attributes. Talk about what basic strokes it contains and which other uppercase letter children see in it. (***P is in R***)

Model Write the letter on guidelines as you say the stroke description. Have the children use their index finger to write **R** on their desktop as you repeat the stroke description and the children say it with you.

Practice Let children practice writing the new letter in centers or at their tables in a variety of ways: on marker boards or slates, on large paper at an easel, in sand or finger paint.

2. Write and Evaluate

Ask children to trace the shaded letters with their finger or pencil, beginning each one at the dot. Then ask them to write a row of letters below the shaded models.

✓ **Stop and Check** This icon directs children to stop and circle the best letter they wrote.

To help them evaluate **R,** ask:
• Is the curved part of your **R** round?
• Are your slide right and slide left strokes about the same?

To help children evaluate **r,** ask:
• Does your **r** begin at the midline?
• Does your push up stroke retrace the pull down stroke?

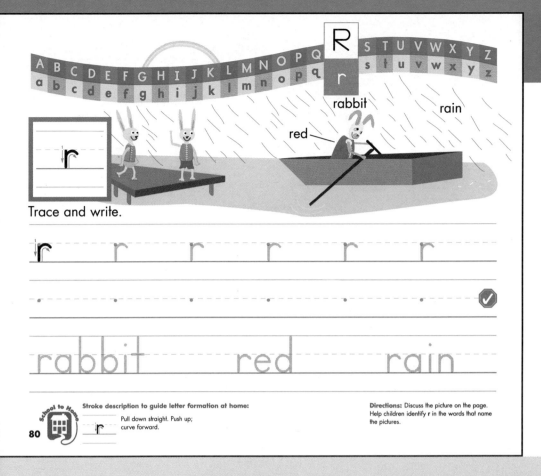

Trace and write.

r   r   r   r   r   r   r

rabbit   red   rain

Stroke description to guide letter formation at home:

r   Pull down straight. Push up;
    curve forward.

Directions: Discuss the picture on the page. Help children identify **r** in the words that name the pictures.

PRACTICE MASTER 52

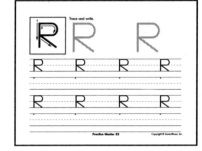

PRACTICE MASTER 53

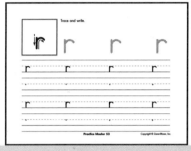

Apply

Ask children to trace the target letter in each shaded word with their finger or pencil. Children who are ready may trace the complete words. Relate the words to the picture at the top of the page.

School to Home

Families may use the stroke descriptions on the student page to encourage good letter formation at home. Copy and distribute **Practice Master 99** for children to take home for more practice.

Fun and Games

 auditory   visual   kinesthetic

Using Manipulatives

Provide an enlarged model of the target letter and a variety of small implements, such as a craft stick, a large marble, a small plastic dinosaur, or a small toy car. Encourage the child to use the implement to trace the basic strokes of the letter. (kinesthetic, visual)

Letter Cards

Make two sets of letter cards using construction paper. Print two cards for each letter. Lay one set in a row on the floor. Scramble the second set and lay them in a row near the first set. Invite children to rearrange the second set to match the first set. Vary this game by changing the shape of the letter cards or the letters used in the game. (visual, kinesthetic)

Phonics Connection

Have fun with the children as you say tongue twisters together. Introduce one, such as *The rabbit ran around the rock,* and have children say it with you. Encourage the children to develop other tongue twisters based on the sound of the target letter. (auditory)

T79

Touch the headline; **pull down straight** to the baseline. Lift. Touch the headline; **slant right** to the baseline. **Push up straight** to the headline.

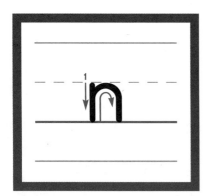

Touch the midline; **pull down straight** to the baseline. **Push up; curve forward** (right); **pull down straight** to the baseline.

Corrective Strategy

To help children make **n** in one continuous motion, demonstrate how all the strokes flow smoothly from one to the other, including the retrace of the first vertical stroke.

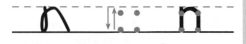

T80

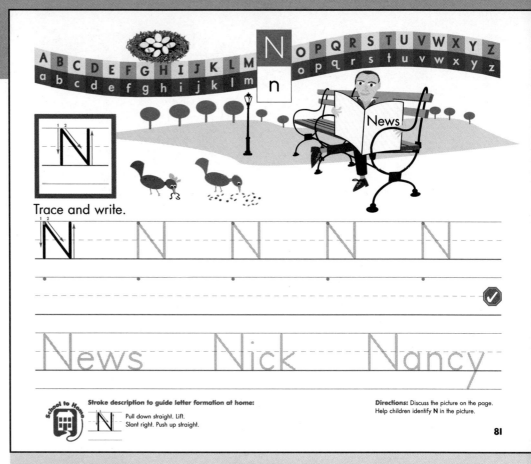

Trace and write.

News Nick Nancy

School to Home **Stroke description to guide letter formation at home:**
Pull down straight. Lift.
Slant right. Push up straight.

Directions: Discuss the picture on the page.
Help children identify **N** in the picture.

81

Use teaching steps 1, 2, and 3 below for pages 81 and 82 in the student book.

1. Present the Letter

Ask children to recognize the target letter in the ABC border and in the picture words. Then have them look at **N** as you help them talk about what basic strokes it contains. (*vertical, slant*)

Model Write the letter on guidelines as you say the stroke description. Model writing it in the air as you repeat the stroke description. Have the children arrange the appropriate Basic Strokes pieces to form the letter, saying the stroke description again with you.

Practice Let children practice writing the new letter in centers or at their tables in a variety of ways: on marker boards or slates, on large paper at an easel, in sand or finger paint.

2. Write and Evaluate

Ask children to trace the shaded letters with their finger or pencil, beginning each one at the dot. Then ask them to write a row of letters below the shaded models.

✓ Stop and Check This icon directs children to stop and circle the best letter they wrote.

To help them evaluate **N,** ask:
• Is your **N** about the same size as the model?
• Are your strokes straight?

To help children evaluate **n,** ask:
• Are your vertical strokes straight?
• Does your **n** fit between the midline and the baseline?

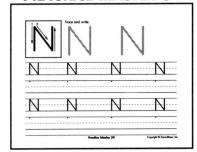

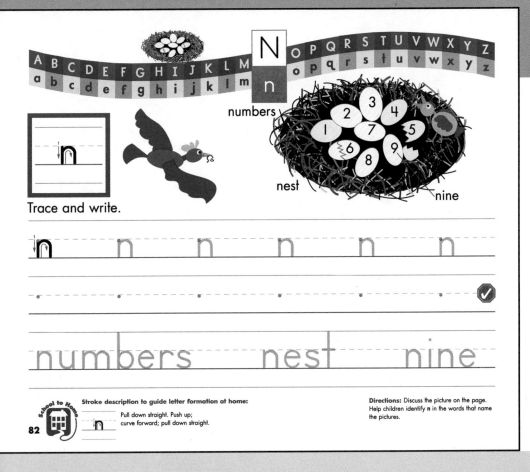

Trace and write.

n   n   n   n   n   n

numbers   nest   nine

Stroke description to guide letter formation at home:

n   Pull down straight. Push up;
     curve forward; pull down straight.

Directions: Discuss the picture on the page. Help children identify **n** in the words that name the pictures.

PRACTICE MASTER 54

Trace and write.

N   N   N

N   N   N   N

N   N   N   N

Practice Master 54   Copyright © Zaner-Bloser, Inc.

PRACTICE MASTER 55

Trace and write.

n   n   n

n   n   n   n

n   n   n   n

Practice Master 55   Copyright © Zaner-Bloser, Inc.

Apply

Ask children to trace the target letter in each shaded word with their finger or pencil. Children who are ready may trace the complete words. Relate the words to the picture at the top of the page.

School to Home

Families may use the stroke descriptions on the student page to encourage good letter formation at home. Copy and distribute **Practice Master 100** for children to take home for more practice.

Readiness Counts!

Vertical Letters

Young children may have difficulty writing letters that are straight up and down, especially letters with slant strokes. They may tend to write letters that tip either left or right. Use the following activities in your classroom to develop the concept of verticality. (See page T7 for characteristics of the pre-writer, the emergent writer, and the developing writer.)

For the Pre-Writer

Have children be vertical lines by lying next to each other on the floor. Use masking tape to make several vertical lines on the floor and have children walk, jump, creep, or skip along the lines—or trace the lines with their toes!

For the Emergent Writer

Use masking tape to form a set of very large guidelines on the floor. Encourage children, singly or in small groups, to position themselves as various letters in place on the guidelines; for example, **L, I, T,** and **N.**

For the Developing Writer

If children make the first stroke in a letter straight, the rest of the letter is more likely to be straight. Provide soft, oversized chalk and have children hold it between the thumb and index finger to practice vertical strokes at the chalkboard. Begin by placing two sets of dots about six inches apart to mark the starting and stopping point of each vertical stroke.

Touch the headline; **pull down straight** to the baseline. Lift. Touch the headline; **slant right** to the baseline. **Slant up** (right) to the headline. **Pull down straight** to the baseline.

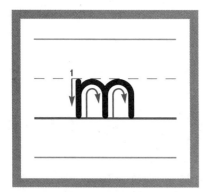

Touch the midline; **pull down straight** to the baseline. **Push up; curve forward** (right); **pull down straight** to the baseline. **Push up; curve forward** (right); **pull down straight** to the baseline.

Alternate Letter Formation

Use this stroke description to show an alternate method for children who have difficulty using the continuous-stroke method.

Pull down straight. Lift. **Slant right**. Lift. **Slant left**. Lift. **Pull down straight**.

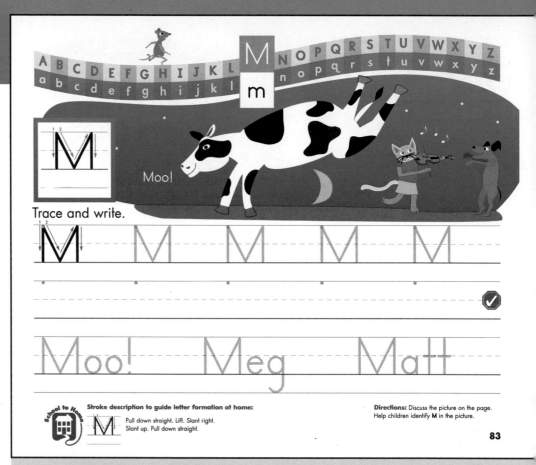

Moo!

Trace and write.

M M M M M

Moo! Meg Matt

Stroke description to guide letter formation at home:

M Pull down straight. Lift. Slant right. Slant up. Pull down straight.

Directions: Discuss the picture on the page. Help children identify **M** in the picture.

83

Use teaching steps 1, 2, and 3 below for pages 83 and 84 in the student book.

1. Present the Letter

Ask children to recognize the target letter in the ABC border and in the picture words. Focus on the letter's shape by helping the children notice that **M** has two vertical strokes and two slant strokes.

Model Write the letter on guidelines as you say the stroke description. Model writing it in the air as you repeat the stroke description. Have the children use the corresponding Basic Strokes pieces to form the letter on their desktop. Then say the description together as they trace the letter.

Practice Let children practice writing the new letter in centers or at their tables in a variety of ways: on marker boards or slates, on large paper at an easel, in sand or finger paint.

2. Write and Evaluate

Ask children to trace the shaded letters with their finger or pencil, beginning each one at the dot. Then ask them to write a row of letters below the shaded models.

Stop and Check This icon directs children to stop and circle the best letter they wrote.

To help them evaluate **M,** ask:
• Are the strokes in your **M** straight?
• Is your **M** about the same size as the model?

To help children evaluate **m,** ask:
• Does your **m** have three pull down straight strokes?
• Are the tops of the curve strokes round?

T82

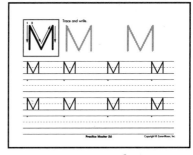

Mm

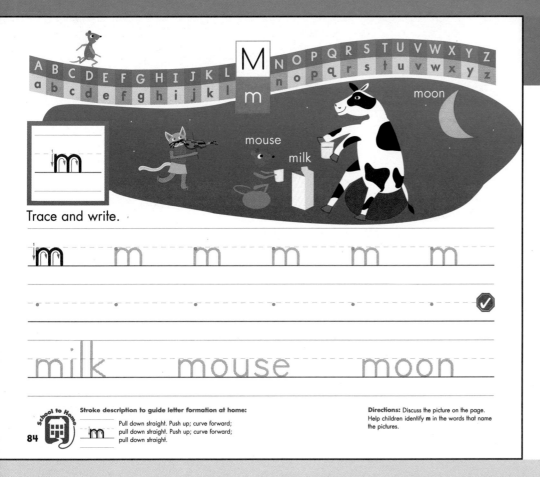

Trace and write.

m   m   m   m   m   m

✓

milk   mouse   moon

PRACTICE MASTER 56

Trace and write.

M   M   M
M   M   M   M
M   M   M   M

Practice Master 56   Copyright © Zaner-Bloser, Inc.

PRACTICE MASTER 57

Trace and write.

m   m   m
m   m   m   m
m   m   m   m

Practice Master 57   Copyright © Zaner-Bloser, Inc.

Apply

Ask children to trace the target letter in each shaded word with their finger or pencil. Children who are ready may trace the complete words. Relate the words to the picture at the top of the page.

Families may use the stroke descriptions on the student page to encourage good letter formation at home. Copy and distribute **Practice Master 101** for children to take home for more practice.

Fun and Games

auditory   visual   kinesthetic

Using Manipulatives Near the art table, display letter cards that correspond to letters you have cut from simple sponges. Invite children to make letters by dipping the sponge letters into paint and printing with them. (visual, kinesthetic)

Letter Bracelets Write different letters on tagboard shapes, punch a hole in each shape, and put each shape on a piece of yarn to make several bracelets. Distribute the bracelets to the children to wear for the day. During the school day, give instructions, such as "Will the children wearing the letter **G** get their coats?" or "All children whose bracelets have the letter **M** should come pick out a book now." (visual, auditory)

Phonics Connection

Write the target letter on the chalkboard. Ask children with names that begin with the target letter to stand. Write each child's name on the board. Ask children to point to the target letter in each name and say the letter's name. Encourage children to say the sound of the letter; for example, for **m** they would say /m/. (auditory, kinesthetic, visual)

T83

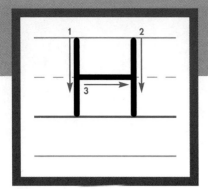

Touch the headline; **pull down straight** to the baseline. Lift. Move to the right and touch the headline; **pull down straight** to the baseline. Lift. Move to the left and touch the midline; **slide right**.

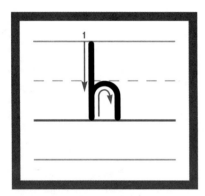

Touch the headline; **pull down straight** to the baseline. **Push up; curve forward** (right); **pull down straight** to the baseline.

Corrective Strategy

Place dots to show children where to write the slide right stroke.

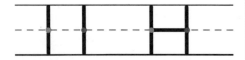

T84

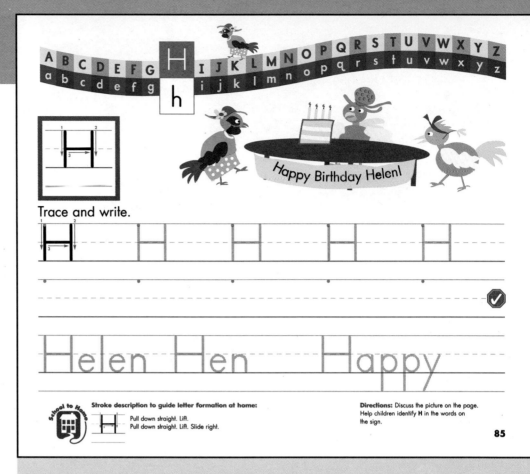

Trace and write.

Happy Birthday Helen!

Helen Hen Happy

Directions: Discuss the picture on the page. Help children identify **H** in the words on the sign.

85

Use teaching steps 1, 2, and 3 below for pages 85 and 86 in the student book.

1. Present the Letter

Ask children to recognize the target letter in the ABC border and in the picture words. Then have them look at **H** as you talk about what basic strokes it contains and what children think it resembles. (*H looks like part of a ladder.*)

Model Write the letter on guidelines as you say the stroke description. Model writing it in the air as you repeat the stroke description. Have the children echo it as they write the letter in the air with you.

Practice Let children practice writing the new letter in centers or at their tables in a variety of ways: on marker boards or slates, on large paper at an easel, in sand or finger paint.

2. Write and Evaluate

Ask children to trace the shaded letters with their finger or pencil, beginning each one at the dot. Then ask them to write a row of letters below the shaded models.

✓ **Stop and Check** This icon directs children to stop and circle the best letter they wrote.

To help them evaluate **H,** ask:
• Does your slide right stroke touch both pull down straight strokes?
• Is your letter wide, and not squeezed together?

To help children evaluate **h,** ask:
• Is your first stroke straight?
• Is the "hump" of your **h** round?

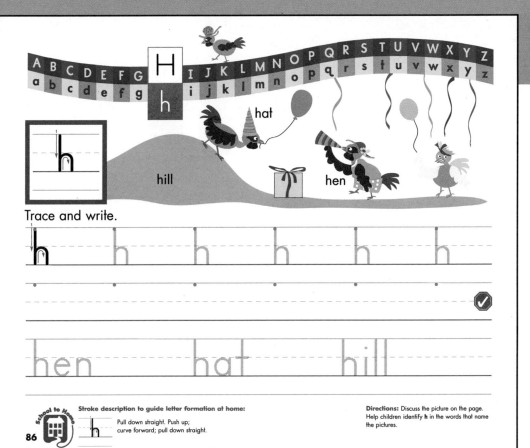

Trace and write.

h h h h h h

hen   hat   hill

School to Home

Stroke description to guide letter formation at home:

h   Pull down straight. Push up; curve forward; pull down straight.

Directions: Discuss the picture on the page. Help children identify **h** in the words that name the pictures.

Hh

PRACTICE MASTER 58

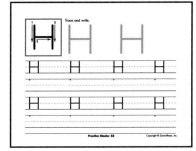

PRACTICE MASTER 59

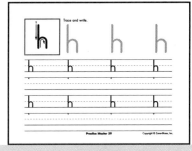

Apply

Ask children to trace the target letter in each word with their finger or pencil. Children who are ready may trace the complete words. Relate the words to the picture at the top of the page.

School to Home

Families may use the stroke descriptions on the student page to encourage good letter formation at home. Copy and distribute **Practice Master 102** for children to take home for more practice.

Readiness Counts!

Spacing

Young children may have difficulty leaving an appropriate amount of space between letters and words in their writing. Use the following activities in your classroom to develop spacing concepts. (See page T7 for characteristics of the pre-writer, the emergent writer, and the developing writer.)

For the Pre-Writer

Encourage children to explore spacing as they play with blocks. When they paint or draw, discuss the spacing of elements in their artwork. As children begin to write lines and letters, emphasize that each must have enough space so that it is not bumped or crowded. Provide space on the chalkboard or on large sheets of blank paper.

For the Emergent Writer

Prepare an empty squeeze bottle of "space" to use in your classroom. Squeeze a little "space" between letters and words as you demonstrate on the chalkboard or observe individual children writing. Explain that each word is a "family" that lives in its own "house." Ask children to draw houses around several words, making a "room" for each letter.

For the Developing Writer

Teach children to leave a one-finger space between words in their writing. Children can use this method to judge spacing as they write and to evaluate the spacing of their finished writing. Left-handed children may find it easier to measure using a "spaceman" made from a narrow craft stick.

Practice

Practice is critical to handwriting success. Each child benefits most from brief periods of practice done in his or her dominant learning modality. Make handwriting practice fun and engaging for children. Try these suggestions.

- Ask 10–12 children to write a target letter on the chalkboard or chart paper. Discuss the letters as a whole-group activity. Talk about which letters are best and why. Then ask everyone to write the letter 3–4 times.

- Read a favorite alphabet book aloud. Ask children to write each letter as it is named in the book.

- Have one partner finger-trace a letter on the other partner's back or palm several times. After the letter is guessed, the partners should switch roles.

Practice

Write the letters.

r r   n n   m m   h h

R   N   M   H

87

---

1. Review the Letters

Write the letters **R, r, N, n, M, m,** and **H, h** on the chalkboard or chart paper. Invite a volunteer to come up and trace each letter you wrote as you repeat its stroke description. Next, give clues that describe one of the letters, such as *This letter is short. It has one "hump."* Invite children to guess the letter. (*n*) Repeat for several more letters.

2. Write and Evaluate

Remind children to check their sitting, paper, and pencil positions. Point out that there are no green starting dots on the page. Ask children if they remember where to begin each letter. Then have them complete student page 87. If time allows, challenge the children to write words that name the pictures on the page.

✓ **Stop and Check** Praise children's progress in writing these letters. Invite volunteers to tell how their writing has improved. To help children evaluate their letters, ask:

- Does your **R** have a good slant line?
- Do the vertical lines in **N** and **M** stand up straight?
- Is your **n** short?
- Does your **H** cross in the middle?

Write the Alphabet

Write the missing lowercase letters.

k

v w x y z

88

Write the Alphabet pages show-case children's ability to write letters from memory. When children write a letter automatically, beginning at the correct starting point and using the correct stroke sequence, they demonstrate that they have successfully formed a clear mental and motor image of the letter.

Using Manipulatives

Using manipulatives during handwriting instruction allows children to see, touch, and demonstrate the way letters are formed. Try some of the following ideas for hands-on handwriting in your classroom.

- Allow children to freely handle and experiment with their Zaner-Bloser Basic Strokes pieces.
- Form letters from clay or fun dough.
- When children are using the uppercase and lowercase alphabet cards from student pages 5–8, challenge them to arrange groups of letters that have similar shapes. Discuss similarities and differences.
- Create a center around Zaner-Bloser's interactive, write-on, wipe-off book *Now I Know My ABCs*.
- Challenge children to form letter shapes from rows of dry beans, buttons, counting bears, craft sticks, or other small pieces.
- Provide a variety of writing tools that interest and motivate children, including chalk, scented markers, glitter glue pens, magic slates, and sheets of newsprint.

Apply

Sing "The Alphabet Song" with children. Ask them to clap or stand up when they hear **r, n, m,** or **h**. You may wish to add a box or highlight to these letters on the lowercase alphabet chart you prepared.

Examine student page 88 with the children. Point out that there are no models on the page that show how to write the letters. Tell children they can show that they really know how to write their letters when they can write them "by heart" without any models.

Ask children to complete the page on their own, writing the missing lowercase letters within the alphabet. Observe whether children are learning how to write these letters automatically and correctly. Celebrate their accomplishment!

Special Helps

To foster eye-hand coordination, prepare cards with patterns of prewriting strokes or simple shapes; for example, OTOTOTO, △ △ △, or □ □ □. Ask the child to use a writing implement or his or her index finger to trace over the lines of each shape. The child can then draw the pattern on paper or the chalkboard. Alternately, provide stencils of simple shapes and ask children to use them to make patterns.

—*Maureen King, O.T.R.*

Touch the headline; **slant right** to the baseline. **Slant up** (right) to the headline.

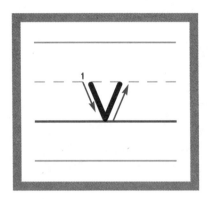

Touch the midline; **slant right** to the baseline. **Slant up** (right) to the midline.

Alternate Letter Formation

Use this stroke description to show an alternate method for children who have difficulty using the continuous-stroke method.

——— **Slant right.** Lift.
V   **Slant left.**

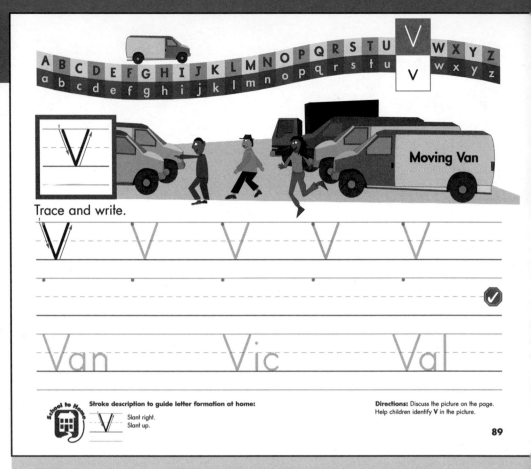

Trace and write.

Van   Vic   Val

School to Home
Stroke description to guide letter formation at home:

Slant right.
Slant up.

Directions: Discuss the picture on the page. Help children identify **V** in the picture.

89

Use teaching steps 1, 2, and 3 below for pages 89 and 90 in the student book.

1. Present the Letter

Ask children to recognize the target letter in the ABC border and in the picture words. Then have them look at **V** as you discuss its shape and attributes. Point out that **V** has two slant strokes that meet at the baseline.

Model Write the letter on guidelines as you say the stroke description. Have the children use two slant strokes from their Basic Strokes pieces to form **V** on their desktop. Have the children say the stroke description with you as they trace the letter.

Practice Let children practice writing the new letter in centers or at their tables in a variety of ways: on marker boards or slates, on large paper at an easel, in sand or finger paint.

2. Write and Evaluate

Ask children to trace the shaded letters with their finger or pencil, beginning each one at the dot. Then ask them to write a row of letters below the shaded models.

 Stop and Check This icon directs children to stop and circle the best letter they wrote.

To help them evaluate **V,** ask:

- Is your **V** about the same size as the model?
- Are your slant strokes straight, and not curved?

To help children evaluate **v,** ask:

- Does your **v** touch both the midline and the baseline?
- Are your slant strokes straight?

T88

Vv

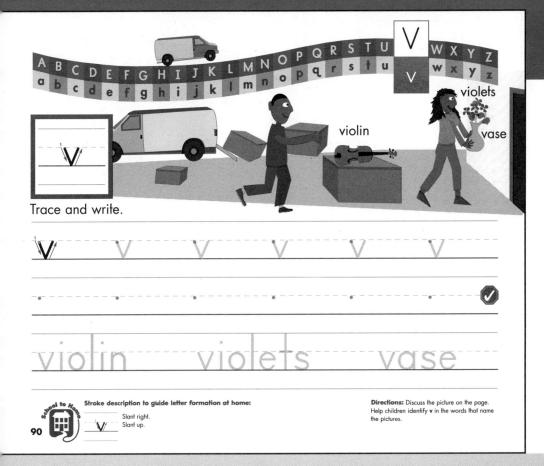

violets

violin

vase

Trace and write.

V   V   V   V   V   V

violin   violets   vase

School to Home

Stroke description to guide letter formation at home:

V Slant right.
   Slant up.

90

Directions: Discuss the picture on the page. Help children identify **v** in the words that name the pictures.

PRACTICE MASTER 60

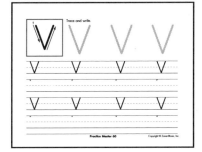

PRACTICE MASTER 61

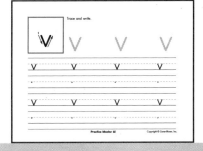

Apply

Ask children to trace the target letter in each shaded word with their finger or pencil. Children who are ready may trace the complete words. Relate the words to the picture at the top of the page.

School to Home

Families may use the stroke descriptions on the student page to encourage good letter formation at home. Copy and distribute **Practice Master 103** for children to take home for more practice.

Fun and Games

auditory   visual   kinesthetic

Using Manipulatives Cut letter shapes in the surface of halved potatoes. Near the art table, display letter cards that correspond to the potato letters. Invite the children to make letters by dipping the surface of the potato letters into paint and printing with them. (visual, kinesthetic)

A Good Story Read a well-known or popular book to the children, such as *"More, More, More," said the Baby: Three Love Stories; Millions of Cats; The Mitten;* or another book of your choice. Then distribute drawing paper that has one row of guidelines pasted at the top. Encourage the children to draw and write about the story.

Phonics Connection

Fill a tray with sand, cornmeal, or another fine-grain material. Then tape record yourself saying familiar words that begin with consonant sounds, such as **van**. Place the materials in a center. Invite children to write the initial letter of each word in the sand as they listen to the tape. (visual, auditory, kinesthetic)

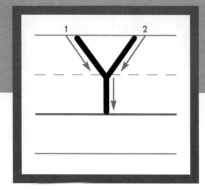

Touch the headline; **slant right** to the midline. Lift. Move to the right and touch the headline; **slant left** to the midline. **Pull down straight** to the baseline.

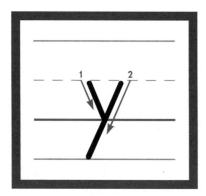

Touch the midline; **slant right** to the baseline. Lift. Move to the right and touch the midline; **slant left** through the baseline.

Corrective Strategy

Write three models of **Y**, each with a different stroke dotted. Have children write or trace as you say the stroke description. Encourage them to stop before making the vertical stroke.

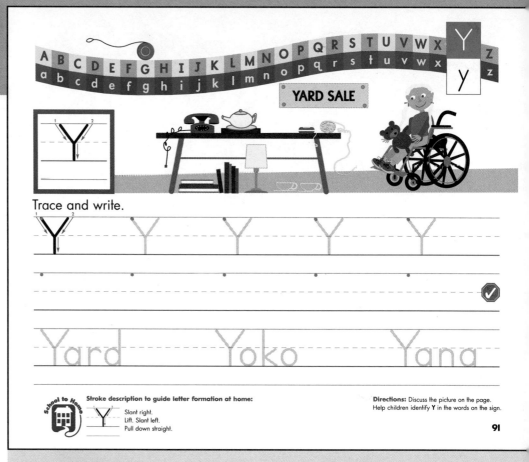

Trace and write.

Yard   Yoko   Yana

School to Home **Stroke description to guide letter formation at home:**

Y Slant right.
   Lift. Slant left.
   Pull down straight.

Directions: Discuss the picture on the page. Help children identify **Y** in the words on the sign.

91

Use teaching steps 1, 2, and 3 below for pages 91 and 92 in the student book.

1. Present the Letter

Ask children to recognize the target letter in the ABC border and in the picture words. Then have them look at the letter as you discuss its shape and attributes. Talk about what basic strokes it contains, and have children select the appropriate strokes from their Basic Strokes pieces and form the letter on their desktop.

Model Write the letter on guidelines as you say the stroke description. Have the children say it with you as they use their index finger to trace the **Y** on their desktop.

Practice Let children practice writing the new letter in centers or at their tables in a variety of ways: on marker boards or slates, on large paper at an easel, in sand or finger paint.

2. Write and Evaluate

Ask children to trace the shaded letters with their finger or pencil, beginning each one at the dot. Then ask them to write a row of letters below the shaded models.

Stop and Check This icon directs children to stop and circle the best letter they wrote.

To help them evaluate **Y,** ask:
- Do your slant strokes meet near the midline?
- Does your **Y** end with a pull down straight stroke?

To help children evaluate **y,** ask:
- Does your slant right stroke stop at the baseline?
- Are your strokes straight and not curved?

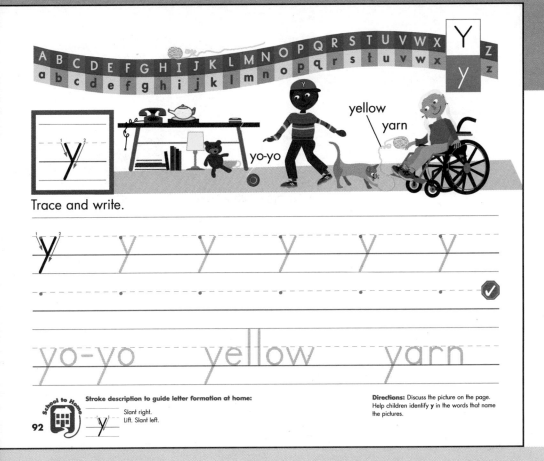

Trace and write.

yo-yo   yellow   yarn

Stroke description to guide letter formation at home:

y   Slant right.
     Lift. Slant left.

Directions: Discuss the picture on the page. Help children identify **y** in the words that name the pictures.

PRACTICE MASTER 62

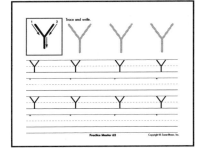

PRACTICE MASTER 63

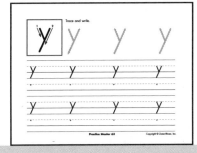

③ Apply

Ask children to trace the target letter in each shaded word with their finger or pencil. Children who are ready may trace the complete words. Relate the words to the picture at the top of the page.

School to Home

Families may use the stroke descriptions on the student page to encourage good letter formation at home. Copy and distribute **Practice Master 104** for children to take home for more practice.

Readiness Counts!

Modality Strengths

Every classroom includes children with varied modality strengths. The sensory mode they use most often influences their classroom behavior and achievement. (See page T7 for characteristics of the pre-writer, the emergent writer, and the developing writer.)

For the Pre-Writer

Have the child form shapes in the air using full-arm movement. (kinesthetic)

Ask children to name the basic strokes that make up a shape as that shape is presented. (auditory)

Provide models of shapes for the child to duplicate. (visual)

For the Emergent Writer

Ask children to walk out the letter strokes on the floor. (kinesthetic)

Have children verbalize each stroke in the letter as that letter is presented. (auditory)

Have children look at each individual stroke carefully before they attempt to write the letter. (visual)

For the Developing Writer

Encourage children to write strokes and letters in sand or a similar medium. (kinesthetic)

Ask children to write random letters as you verbalize the strokes. (auditory)

Have children look at the letter as a whole and ask themselves questions about whether the letter is tall or short, fat or skinny, and what kinds of strokes it contains. (visual)

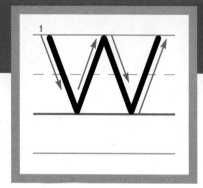

Touch the headline; **slant right** to the baseline. **Slant up** (right) to the headline. **Slant right** to the baseline. **Slant up** (right) to the headline.

Touch the midline; **slant right** to the baseline. **Slant up** (right) to the midline. **Slant right** to the baseline. **Slant up** (right) to the midline.

Alternate Letter Formation

Use this stroke description to show an alternate method for children who have difficulty using the continuous-stroke method.

 Slant right. Lift. **Slant left**. Lift. **Slant right**. Lift. **Slant left** to the baseline.

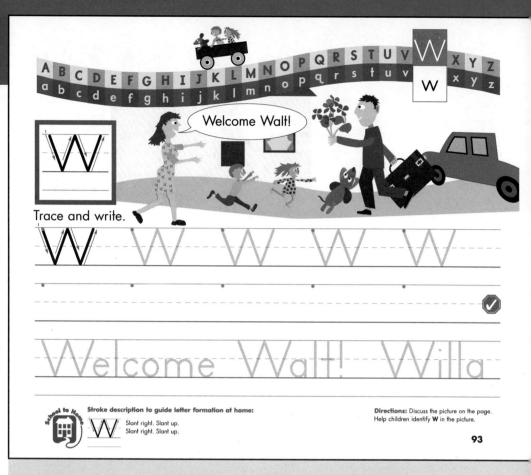

Welcome Walt!

Trace and write.

Welcome Walt! Willa

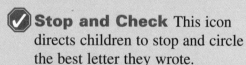

Stroke description to guide letter formation at home:

Slant right. Slant up.
Slant right. Slant up.

Directions: Discuss the picture on the page. Help children identify **W** in the picture.

93

Use teaching steps 1, 2, and 3 below for pages 93 and 94 in the student book.

1. Present the Letter

Ask children to recognize the target letter in the ABC border and in the picture words. Help them notice that **W** is formed with two **V**'s. Encourage children to use four of the orange slant strokes in their Basic Strokes set to form the letter over the book model.

Model Write the letter on guidelines as you say the stroke description. Model writing it in the air as you repeat the stroke description. Have the children say it as they trace the letter in the model box on the page in their books.

Practice Let children practice writing the new letter in centers or at their tables in a variety of ways: on marker boards or slates, on large paper at an easel, in sand or finger paint.

2. Write and Evaluate

Ask children to trace the shaded letters with their finger or pencil, beginning each one at the dot. Then ask them to write a row of letters below the shaded models.

Stop and Check This icon directs children to stop and circle the best letter they wrote.

To help them evaluate **W,** ask:

- Does your **W** have four straight slant strokes?
- Is your **W** about the same size as the model?

To help children evaluate **w,** ask:

- Are the strokes in your **w** straight?
- Does your **w** rest on the baseline?

T92

Ww

Trace and write.

wagon   wheel   window

94

Stroke description to guide letter formation at home:

Ww   Slant right. Slant up.
Slant right. Slant up.

Directions: Discuss the picture on the page. Help children identify **w** in the words that name the pictures.

PRACTICE MASTER 64

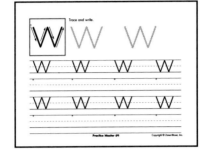

PRACTICE MASTER 65

Apply

Ask children to trace the target letter in each shaded word with their finger or pencil. Children who are ready may trace the complete words. Relate the words to the picture at the top of the page.

School to Home

Families may use the stroke descriptions on the student page to encourage good letter formation at home. Copy and distribute **Practice Master 105** for children to take home for more practice.

Fun and Games

auditory   visual   kinesthetic

Using Manipulatives Have the children select a card from their alphabet letter card sets. (See pages T4 and T5.) Then have them find the corresponding strokes in their Basic Strokes pieces. Ask them to use the strokes to form the letter beside the model on the card. (visual, kinesthetic)

Come Back to the Circle

Give each child an index card with a letter printed on it. Then have the children scatter to different parts of the classroom. Hold up a large construction paper letter for the children to see. Have the child who is holding the matching index card identify the letter and return to the circle area. (visual)

Phonics Connection

Distribute index cards with guidelines. After everyone agrees that *worm* begins with **w,** ask children to write a word that begins with **w** on each card. Encourage them to use words from the student page or other words they know. Arrange the cards to form a word worm, and see how long the children can make the worm. Say the words together, emphasizing the initial /w/ sound. (visual, kinesthetic)

Practice

Practice is critical to handwriting success. Each child benefits most from brief periods of practice done in his or her dominant learning modality. Practice activities that provide meaningful purposes for writing are best. Try these suggestions.

• Establish a working post office in your classroom. Provide a cardboard mail box, stationery, and sticker "stamps" or use Zaner-Bloser's *Post Office Kit*. Allow time each day for children to write letters and for the mail to be delivered.

• Write a child's story as he or she dictates to you. Then examine the written story together, selecting 2–3 words for the child to write and practice. Have the child illustrate the story and place it in the class library.

• Challenge teams of 3–4 students to form a target letter with their bodies on a classroom rug. Other children can guess the letter and discuss how it is formed.

Practice

Write the letters.

V   V   Y   Y   W   W

V   V   Y   Y   W   W

95

1 Review the Letters

Write the letters **V, v, Y, y,** and **W, w** on the chalkboard or chart paper. Invite a volunteer to come up and trace each letter you wrote as you repeat its stroke description. Next, give clues that describe one of the letters, such as *This letter looks like lowercase v with a tail. It is written with two strokes.* (**y**) Repeat for several more letters.

2 Write and Evaluate

Remind children to check their sitting, paper, and pencil positions. Point out that there are no green starting dots on the page. Ask children if they remember where to begin each letter. Then have them complete student page 95. If time allows, challenge the children to write words that name the pictures on the page.

✓ **Stop and Check** Praise children's progress in writing these letters. To help children evaluate their letters, ask:

• Does each letter have the right number of slant lines?
• Do your **v** and **V** look the same except for size?
• Is your **Y** tall?
• Did you write **w** with straight lines?

T94

Write the Alphabet

Write the missing uppercase letters.

K

X   Z

96

Write the Alphabet pages showcase children's ability to write letters from memory. When children write a letter automatically, beginning at the correct starting point and using the correct stroke sequence, they demonstrate that they have successfully formed a clear mental and motor image of the letter.

 ## Using Manipulatives

Using manipulatives during handwriting instruction allows children to see, touch, and demonstrate the way letters are formed. Try some of the following ideas for hands-on handwriting in your classroom.

- Allow children to freely handle and experiment with their Zaner-Bloser Basic Strokes pieces.
- Provide Zaner-Bloser *Touch and Trace Letter Cards* for letter practice.
- Create a "letter town" with letter-shaped block buildings.
- Touch and trace large magnetic letters.
- Use tagboard and a hole punch to make a sewing card for each letter. Provide shoelaces for lacing.
- Challenge children to form letter shapes from rows of dry beans, buttons, counting bears, craft sticks, or other small pieces.
- Provide a variety of writing tools that interest and motivate children, including chalk, scented markers, glitter glue pens, magic slates, and sheets of newsprint.

Apply

Sing "The Alphabet Song" with children. Ask them to clap or stand up when they hear **V, Y,** or **W.** You may wish to add a box or highlight to these letters on the uppercase alphabet chart you prepared.

Examine student page 96 with the children. Point out that there are no models on the page that show how to write the letters. Tell children they can show that they really know how to write their letters when they can write them "by heart" without any models.

Ask children to complete the page on their own, writing the missing uppercase letters within the alphabet. Observe whether children are learning how to write these letters automatically and correctly. Celebrate their accomplishment!

Special Helps

Drawing or writing on a vertical surface facilitates development and strengthening of the wrist, hand, and shoulder. It allows gravity to position the wrist correctly for writing. Allow children to color or complete worksheets at about face level on an easel or chalkboard. Small magnets or clips can be used to secure the paper. The back end of the writing instrument should always be visible to the child—mark it with a sticker or smiley face. Check children's writing position frequently, especially as they become fatigued.

—*Maureen King, O.T.R.*

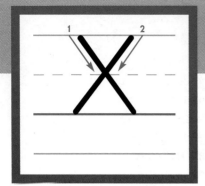

Touch the headline; **slant right** to the baseline. Lift. Move to the right and touch the headline; **slant left** to the baseline.

Touch the midline; **slant right** to the baseline. Lift. Move to the right and touch the midline; **slant left** to the baseline.

Corrective Strategy

Remind children to aim the second stroke in **X** so that it crosses the first stroke near the midline. Place a dot where the slant left should begin.

T96

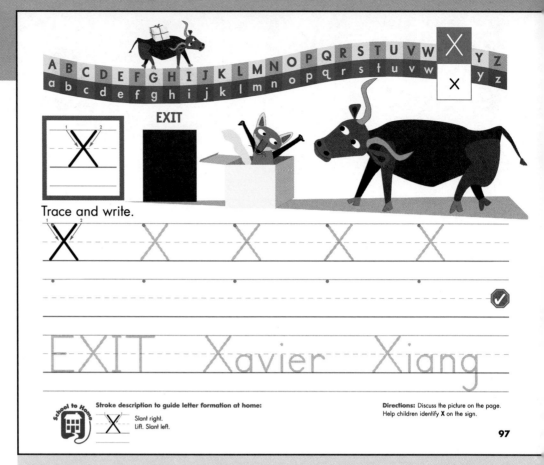

Trace and write.

Use teaching steps 1, 2, and 3 below for pages 97 and 98 in the student book.

School to Home

Stroke description to guide letter formation at home:

X Slant right.
Lift. Slant left.

Directions: Discuss the picture on the page. Help children identify **X** on the sign.

97

1 Present the Letter

Ask children to recognize the target letter in the ABC border and in the picture words. Then have them look at **X** as you talk about what basic strokes it contains. Help children notice that **X** and **x** are the same shape, but have different sizes.

Model Write the letter on guidelines as you say the stroke description. Model writing it in the air as you repeat the stroke description. Have the children say it as they write the letter in the air with you.

Practice Let children practice writing the new letter in centers or at their tables in a variety of ways: on marker boards or slates, on large paper at an easel, in sand or finger paint.

2 Write and Evaluate

Ask children to trace the shaded letters with their finger or pencil, beginning each one at the dot. Then ask them to write a row of letters below the shaded models.

Stop and Check This icon directs children to stop and circle the best letter they wrote.

To help them evaluate **X,** ask:
- Are your slant strokes straight, and not curved?
- Do your slant strokes cross near the midline?

To help children evaluate **x,** ask:
- Are your slant strokes straight, and not curved?
- Does your **x** touch the midline and baseline?

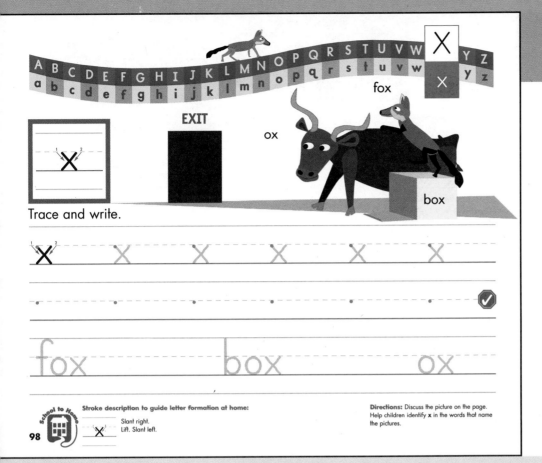

EXIT

fox

ox

box

Trace and write.

fox   box   ox

Directions: Discuss the picture on the page. Help children identify **x** in the words that name the pictures.

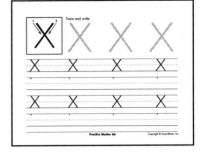

Trace and write.

Practice Master 66   Copyright © Zaner-Bloser, Inc.

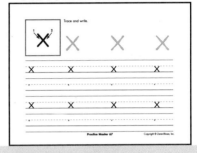

Trace and write.

Practice Master 67   Copyright © Zaner-Bloser, Inc.

 Apply

Ask children to trace the target letter in each shaded word with their finger or pencil. Children who are ready may trace the complete words. Relate the words to the picture at the top of the page.

 School to Home

Families may use the stroke descriptions on the student page to encourage good letter formation at home. Copy and distribute **Practice Master 106** for children to take home for more practice.

Readiness Counts!

Practice

Regular handwriting practice is essential for young writers. Try these ideas for making the most of practice time. (See page T7 for characteristics of the pre-writer, the emergent writer, and the developing writer.)

For the Pre-Writer

Allow time for children to practice forming basic strokes (vertical, horizontal, circle, and slant lines) while painting, drawing, writing at the chalkboard, and fingerwriting in sand. Emphasize large, smooth top-to-bottom and left-to-right strokes as well as proper starting places for circles and slants.

For the Emergent Writer

Asking children to write letters too many times in isolation invites careless, incorrectly formed letters. Instead, demonstrate the correct formation of a letter and then ask children to write it three times on practice paper. Ask them to circle their best letter and tell why it is the best.

For the Developing Writer

Plan practice activities that allow children to write for a purpose. Writing signs, letters and notes, labels, and alphabet books helps children understand that writing is for communication. Make handwriting practice fun by providing a variety of tools such as scented markers, sidewalk chalk, slates, marker boards, and MagnaDoodles.

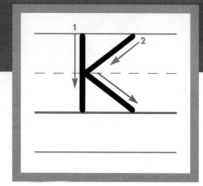

Touch the headline; **pull down straight** to the baseline. Lift. Move to the right and touch the headline; **slant left** to the midline. **Slant right** to the baseline.

Touch the headline; **pull down straight** to the baseline. Lift. Move to the right and touch the midline; **slant left**. **Slant right** to the baseline.

Corrective Strategy

Show how the slant left stroke in **K** stops near the midline where the slant right begins. Place dots to show the width of **K**.

T98

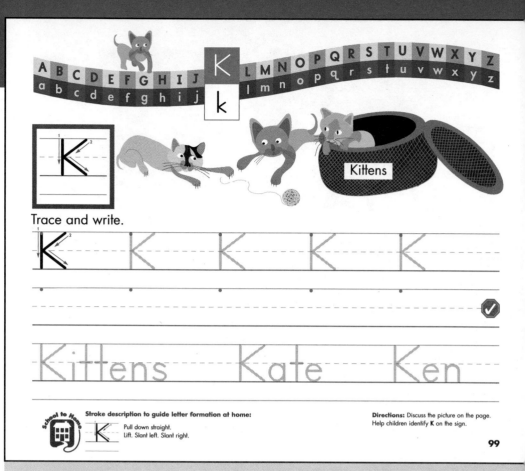

Trace and write.

Kittens   Kate   Ken

Stroke description to guide letter formation at home:

K Pull down straight.
Lift. Slant left. Slant right.

Directions: Discuss the picture on the page.
Help children identify **K** on the sign.

99

Use teaching steps 1, 2, and 3 below for pages 99 and 100 in the student book.

1. Present the Letter

Ask children to recognize the target letter in the ABC border and in the picture words. Have them find the card for **K** in their Uppercase Alphabet Cards. (See pages T4 and T5.) Talk about what strokes it contains and how the strokes fit together to form the letter.

Model Write the letter on guidelines as you say the stroke description. Model writing it in the air as you repeat the stroke description. Have the children say it with you as they trace the letter on the alphabet card.

Practice Let children practice writing the new letter in centers or at their tables in a variety of ways: on marker boards or slates, on large paper at an easel, in sand or finger paint.

2. Write and Evaluate

Ask children to trace the shaded letters with their finger or pencil, beginning each one at the dot. Then ask them to write a row of letters below the shaded models.

Stop and Check This icon directs children to stop and circle the best letter they wrote.

To help them evaluate **K,** ask:
• Do your two slant strokes meet near the midline?
• Is your **K** written straight up and down?

To help children evaluate **k,** ask:
• Are your strokes straight, and not curved?
• Is your **k** straight up and down?

Kk

Trace and write.

kite   key   king

100

Directions: Discuss the picture on the page. Help children identify **k** in the words that name the pictures.

PRACTICE MASTER 68

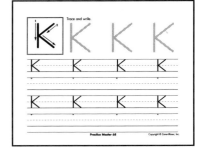

PRACTICE MASTER 69

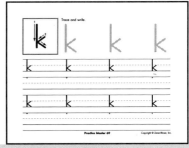

---

3 Apply

Ask children to trace the target letter in each shaded word with their finger or pencil. Children who are ready may trace the complete words. Relate the words to the picture at the top of the page.

School to Home

Families may use the stroke descriptions on the student page to encourage good letter formation at home. Copy and distribute **Practice Master 107** for children to take home for more practice.

Fun and Games

auditory   visual   kinesthetic

Using Manipulatives

Distribute pieces of construction paper or tagboard and a handful of corn kernels to each child. Have the children use glue to highlight the strokes of **K** and then place kernels of corn to cover the letter. (kinesthetic, visual)

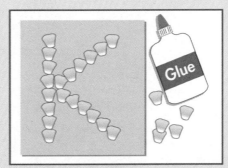

Moving As children's motor skills advance, their handwriting will improve. As a creative movement activity, ask the children to do pretend actions such as these:

paddle a kayak
kick balloons
jump like kangaroos
walk like an elephant
stretch like a cat
sway like a tree

(auditory, kinesthetic)

Phonics Connection

Have children point to each picture on the **K/k** pages in their books as you name it. To focus attention on recognizing sounds and letters, ask a volunteer to choose one picture word and to name all the letters. Then ask if anyone can guess which word was chosen. (visual, auditory)

Touch the headline; **slide right. Slant left** to the baseline. **Slide right**.

Touch the midline; **slide right. Slant left** to the baseline. **Slide right**.

Corrective Strategy

To help children write **Z** with straight lines, demonstrate how to pause before and after the slant left stroke.

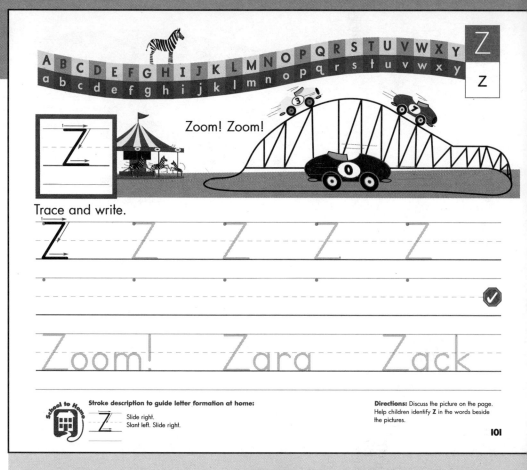

Zoom! Zoom!

Trace and write.

Zoom! Zara Zack

Stroke description to guide letter formation at home:

Z Slide right.
   Slant left. Slide right.

Directions: Discuss the picture on the page. Help children identify **Z** in the words beside the pictures.

101

Use teaching steps 1, 2, and 3 below for pages 101 and 102 in the student book.

1. Present the Letter

Ask children to recognize the target letter in the ABC border and in the picture words. Then have them look at **Z** as you discuss its shape. Talk about what basic strokes it contains. Have children select the strokes from their set of Basic Strokes and form the letter on their desktop.

Model Write the letter on guidelines as you say the stroke description. Model writing it in the air as you repeat the stroke description. Have the children say it with you as they trace the letter on their desktop.

Practice Let children practice writing the new letter in centers or at their tables in a variety of ways: on marker boards or slates, on large paper at an easel, in sand or finger paint.

2. Write and Evaluate

Ask children to trace the shaded letters with their finger or pencil, beginning each one at the dot. Then ask them to write a row of letters below the shaded models.

✓ Stop and Check This icon directs children to stop and circle the best letter they wrote.

To help them evaluate **Z,** ask:
- Is your **Z** about the same size as the model?
- Are your lines straight?

To help children evaluate **z,** ask:
- Are the top and bottom strokes of your **z** about the same?
- Are the top and bottom strokes written right above and below each other?

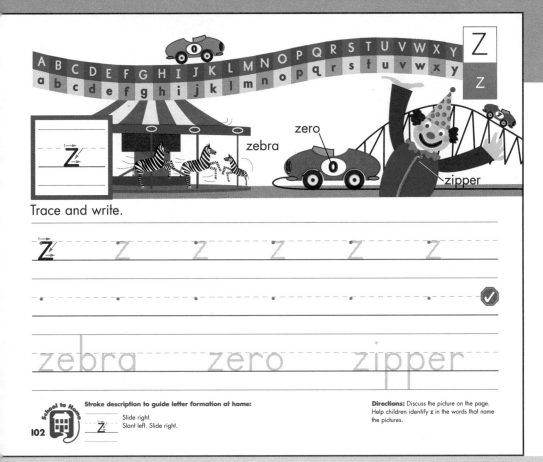

Trace and write.

zebra zero zipper

Directions: Discuss the picture on the page. Help children identify **z** in the words that name the pictures.

PRACTICE MASTER 70

Trace and write.

Z Z Z Z

Z Z Z Z

Z Z Z Z

Practice Master 70   Copyright © Zaner-Bloser, Inc.

PRACTICE MASTER 71

Trace and write.

Z̄ Z Z Z

Z Z Z Z

Z Z Z Z

Practice Master 71   Copyright © Zaner-Bloser, Inc.

Apply

Ask children to trace the target letter in each shaded word with their finger or pencil. Children who are ready may trace the complete words. Relate the words to the picture at the top of the page.

Families may use the stroke descriptions on the student page to encourage good letter formation at home. Copy and distribute **Practice Master 108** for children to take home for more practice.

Readiness Counts!

Fine Motor Skills

In order to write and draw efficiently, the child must have the ability to separate the function of the two sides of the hand. Use the following activities in your classroom to develop this ability. (See page T7 for characteristics of the pre-writer, the emergent writer, and the developing writer.)

For the Pre-Writer

If the child positions the pencil across the palm or all four fingertips to write, provide scissors and help him or her refine scissors skills. Initially, just have the child practice the opening and closing of the scissor blades. If he or she has difficulty keeping the ring and lit-

tle fingers bent and motionless, have him or her hold a small object, such as a piece of soft sponge, with those two fingers pressed against the palm of the hand.

For the Emergent Writer

When the child can "work" the scissors correctly, provide plastic drinking straws for him or her to cut into tiny pieces. If necessary, continue having him or her hold the sponge while carrying out the cutting action.

For the Developing Writer

As the child's expertise improves, provide a variety of materials to cut; for example, manila folders, old playing cards, and cards from magazine ad inserts. As the scissors skills improve, so will the child's ability to hold and use writing implements efficiently.

Practice

auditory visual kinesthetic

Practice is critical to handwriting success. Each child benefits most from brief periods of practice done in his or her dominant learning modality. Practice activities that provide meaningful purposes for writing are best. Try these suggestions.

- Work together as a class to create an alphabet book to share with next year's class. Determine whether the book will feature uppercase letters, lowercase letters, or both. Decide how the book will be illustrated. Assign children to create different pages of the book.

- Write *Handwriting Super Star* at the top of a sheet of paper. Duplicate for each child. Have children write all the letters of the alphabet on the page, using their best handwriting. Send the page home with a note encouraging parents to celebrate the child's accomplishment.

- Invite volunteers to stand and write a letter in the air several times. The rest of the class can guess the letter and write it on paper.

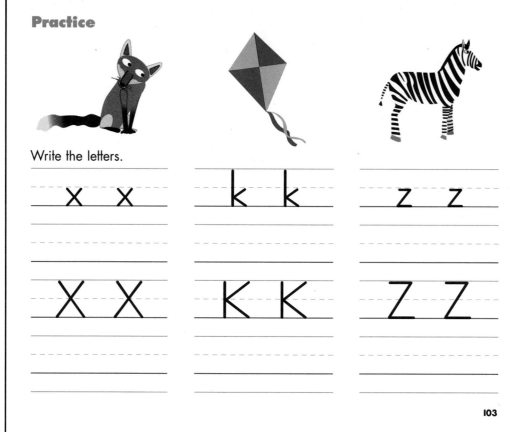

Practice

Write the letters.

x x   k k   z z

X X   K K   Z Z

103

1. Review the Letters

Write the letters **X, x, K, k,** and **Z, z** on the chalkboard or chart paper. Invite a volunteer to come up and trace each letter you wrote as you repeat its stroke description. Next, give clues that describe one of the letters, such as *This letter has two slant strokes that cross each other in the center. It is tall.* (*X*) Repeat for several more letters.

2. Write and Evaluate

Remind children to check their sitting, paper, and pencil positions. Point out that there are no green starting dots on the page. Ask children if they remember where to begin each letter. Then have them complete student page 103. If time allows, challenge the children to write words that name the pictures on the page.

✓ **Stop and Check** Invite volunteers to tell how their writing has improved. To help children evaluate their letters, ask:

- Do your slant strokes in **x** and **X** cross in the middle?
- Do your slant lines touch the vertical line in **k**?
- Is your **K** not too skinny or too fat—about the same width as the model?
- Are your **Z** and **z** the same except for size?

Write the Alphabet

Write the lowercase alphabet.

Write the Alphabet

Write the Alphabet pages showcase children's ability to write letters from memory. When children write a letter automatically, beginning at the correct starting point and using the correct stroke sequence, they demonstrate that they have successfully formed a clear mental and motor image of the letter.

Using Manipulatives

Using manipulatives during handwriting instruction allows children to see, touch, and demonstrate the way that letters are formed. Try some of the following ideas for hands-on handwriting in your classroom.

- When children are using the uppercase and lowercase alphabet cards from student pages 5–8, challenge them to arrange groups of letters that have similar shapes. Discuss similarities and differences.
- Create a center around Zaner-Bloser's interactive, write-on, wipe-off book *Now I Know My ABCs.*
- Assemble edible letters from an assortment of fruit and vegetable pieces.
- Provide Zaner-Bloser *Touch and Trace Letter Cards* for letter practice.
- Create a "letter town" with letter-shaped block buildings.
- Touch and trace large magnetic letters.
- Use tagboard and a hole punch to make a sewing card for each letter. Provide shoelaces for lacing.
- Challenge children to form letter shapes from rows of dry beans, buttons, counting bears, craft sticks, or other small pieces.

Apply

Sing "The Alphabet Song" with children. Ask them to clap or stand up when they hear **x, k,** and **z.** You may wish to add a box or highlight to these letters on the lowercase alphabet chart you prepared. Point out that children have now learned to write all the letters.

Examine student page 104 with the children. Tell children they can show that they really know how to write their letters when they can write them "by heart" without any models.

Ask children to complete the page on their own, writing the entire lowercase alphabet on the lines. Observe whether children are learning how to write letters automatically and correctly. Celebrate their accomplishment!

Special Helps

When children are using markers, ask them to place a marker cap in the fist of the writing hand. Then challenge them to move or "inchworm" it from within the fist to between the thumb and forefinger without assistance from the non-writing hand. When the child performs this task easily, have him or her reverse the motion, moving the marker cap from the thumb and forefinger back into the closed fist.

Additionally, have the child cap the marker using only the thumb and fingertips, to build finger strength. The "click" of the cap provides auditory feedback.

—*Maureen King, O.T.R.*

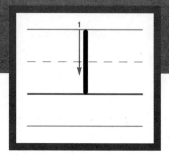

Touch the headline; **pull down straight** to the baseline.

Touch below the headline; **curve forward** (right); **slant left** to the baseline. **Slide right**.

Touch below the headline; **curve forward** (right) to the midline; **curve forward** (right), ending above the baseline.

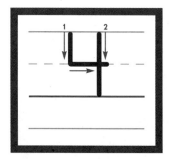

Touch the headline; **pull down straight** to the midline. **Slide right**. Lift. Move to the right and touch the headline; **pull down straight** to the baseline.

T104

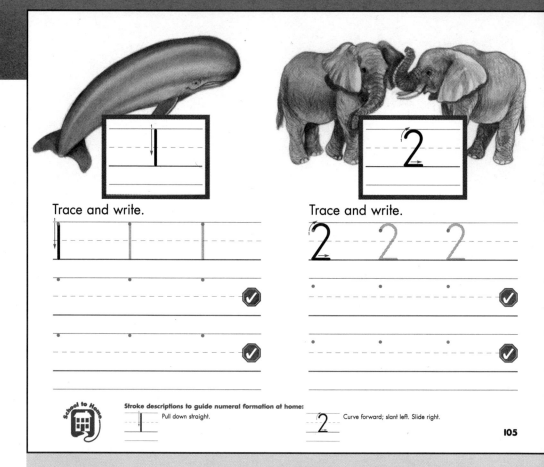

Trace and write.

Trace and write.

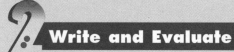
Stroke descriptions to guide numeral formation at home:
Pull down straight.   Curve forward; slant left. Slide right.

105

Use teaching steps 1, 2, and 3 below for pages 105 and 106 in the student book.

1. Present the Numerals

Ask children to recognize each target numeral in the model box at the top of the student page. Talk about what basic strokes it contains and what children think it resembles (e.g., *1 looks like a stick or a lowercase l*).

Model Write each numeral on guidelines as you say the stroke description. Model writing it in the air as you repeat the stroke description. Have the children say it as they write the numeral in the air with you.

Practice Let children practice writing the new numerals in centers or at their tables in a variety of ways: on marker boards or slates, on large paper at an easel, in sand or finger paint.

2. Write and Evaluate

Ask children to trace the shaded numerals with their finger or pencil, beginning each one at the dot. Then ask them to write two rows of numerals below the shaded models.

✓ **Stop and Check** This icon directs children to stop and circle the best numeral they wrote.

To help them evaluate **1,** ask:
• Is the vertical stroke in your **1** straight?

Repeat teaching steps 1 and 2 for numerals 2–4.

To help them evaluate **2–4,** ask:
• Is the slant left stroke in your **2** straight?
• Are both parts of your **3** about the same size?
• Is the slide right stroke in your **4** on the midline?

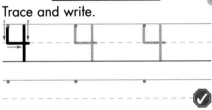

Trace and write.

3   3   3

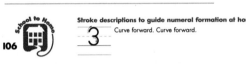

Trace and write.

4   4   4

Stroke descriptions to guide numeral formation at home:

3 — Curve forward. Curve forward.

4 — Pull down straight. Slide right. Lift.
Pull down straight.

106

PRACTICE MASTER 72

Numerals 1-2
Start at the dot. Trace and write 1.

Trace and write 2.
2   2   2   2   2   2

Practice Master 72   Copyright © Zaner-Bloser, Inc.

PRACTICE MASTER 73

Numerals 3-4
Trace and write 3.
3   3   3   3   3   3

Trace and write 4.
4   4   4   4   4   4

Practice Master 73   Copyright © Zaner-Bloser, Inc.

Corrective Strategy

All numerals are tall and touch the headline and the baseline.

2   not   2

Note: Help the children notice that for each new numeral they encounter on the student pages, the illustration includes that number of animals. Also make them aware that the animals in the numeral illustrations become consecutively smaller, from the large whale for **1** to the little chipmunks for **10**.

Fun and Games

auditory   visual   kinesthetic

Using Manipulatives Make sets of objects the children can match and sort. One set might include two or more of each of these items: pencils, blocks, clothespins, dominoes, crayons. Have the children lay out a single row of the items and then place matching items next to the original. Ask children to count the objects and write the corresponding numerals. (visual, kinesthetic)

Threes A triangle has three corners (angles) and three sides (lines). Provide construction paper for the background, and have children use different kinds and sizes of triangles cut from colored construction paper to make a design on the background paper. Ask children to write **3** inside each triangle. (visual, kinesthetic)

Creative Movement Divide the class into groups of four-legged animals (horses, cats, turtles, lions, elephants, rabbits). On a signal, ask each group to move as its animal while the others try to guess the animal's identity. Ask counting questions such as "How many trunks does an elephant have? How many ears does a rabbit have?" (visual, kinesthetic, auditory)

T105

Touch the headline; **pull down straight** to the midline. **Circle forward** (right), ending above the baseline. Lift. Touch the headline; **slide right**.

Touch the headline; **curve down** to the baseline; **curve up** to the midline and around to close the circle.

Touch the headline; **slide right**. **Slant left** to the baseline.

Touch below the headline; **curve back** (left); **curve forward** (right), touching the baseline; **slant up** (right) to the headline.

TI06

Trace and write.

Trace and write.

Stroke descriptions to guide numeral formation at home:

5 — Pull down straight. Circle forward. Lift. Slide right.

6 — Curve down. Curve up and around.

107

Use teaching steps 1, 2, and 3 below for pages 107 and 108 in the student book.

1. Present the Numerals

Ask children to recognize each target numeral in the model box at the top of the student page. Then have them look at the numeral as you discuss its shape and attributes. Talk about what basic strokes it contains and what children think it resembles (e.g., 5 *looks much like an uppercase S*).

Model Write each numeral on guidelines as you say the stroke description. Model writing it in the air as you repeat the stroke description. Have the children say it as they write the numeral in the air with you.

Practice Let children practice writing the new numerals in centers or at their tables in a variety of ways: on marker boards or slates, on large paper at an easel, in sand or finger paint.

2. Write and Evaluate

Ask children to trace the shaded numerals with their finger or pencil, beginning each one at the dot. Then ask them to write two rows of numerals below the shaded models.

Stop and Check This icon directs children to stop and circle the best numeral they wrote.

To help them evaluate **5**, ask:
• Is your **5** straight up and down?

Repeat teaching steps 1 and 2 for numerals 6–8.

To help them evaluate **6–8**, ask:
• Does your **6** have a closed circle?
• Are both strokes of your **7** straight, and not curved?
• Are the curves of your **8** about the same size?

Trace and write.

7 7 7 7

Trace and write.

8 8 8

Stroke descriptions to guide numeral formation at home:

7 Slide right. Slant left.

8 Curve back; curve forward. Slant up.

108

PRACTICE MASTER 74
PRACTICE MASTER 75

Corrective Strategies

The circle in **6** is closed.

6 not 6

The top and bottom parts of **8** are nearly equal.

8 not 8

Fun and Games

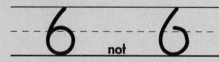

auditory visual kinesthetic

Using Manipulatives

Insects have six legs. Some insects include: ladybugs, grasshoppers, butterflies, ants, and bees. Provide drawing paper and paint. Have the children dip their thumb in the paint and make thumbprints on the paper. Then have them use crayons or markers to add legs and other features to the bugs. Encourage children to add numerals that describe different parts of their pictures. (visual, kinesthetic)

Playful Puppies Give each child a sheet of paper with seven puppies drawn on it. Distribute seven paper bone shapes to each child. Have children match the puppies with the bones to reinforce counting on a one-to-one basis. (visual, kinesthetic)

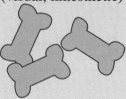

Creative Movement Ask the children to be kangaroos and hop about the room, or to be kittens playing with a ball of yarn. Alternately, teach this cheer:

2-4-6-8;
Who do we appreciate?!

Have the children pretend to lead the crowd at a big game using that cheer. (visual, kinesthetic, auditory)

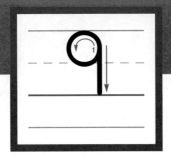

Touch below the headline; **circle back** (left) all the way around. **Pull down straight** to the baseline.

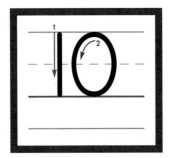

Touch the headline; **pull down straight** to the baseline. Lift. Touch the headline; **curve down** to the baseline; **curve up** to the headline.

Corrective Strategies

The pull down straight stroke in **9** is vertical.

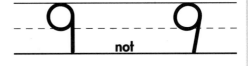

The numeral **10** touches both the headline and baseline.

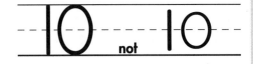

Trace and write.

Trace and write.

Stroke descriptions to guide numeral formation at home:
9 — Circle back all the way around. Pull down straight.
10 — Pull down straight. Lift. Curve down; curve up.

109

Use teaching steps 1 and 2 below for page 109 in the student book.

1. Present the Numerals

Ask the children to recognize each target numeral in the model box at the top of the student page. Then have them look at the numeral as you discuss its shape and attributes. Talk about what basic strokes it contains and what children think it resembles (e.g., *9 looks much like lowercase q*).

Model Write each numeral on guidelines as you say the stroke description. Model writing it in the air as you repeat the stroke description. Have the children say it as they write the numeral in the air with you.

Practice Let children practice writing the new numerals in centers or at their tables in a variety of ways: on marker boards or slates, on large paper at an easel, in sand or finger paint.

2. Write and Evaluate

Ask children to trace the shaded numerals with their finger or pencil, beginning each one at the dot. Then ask them to write two rows of numerals below the shaded models.

✓ **Stop and Check** This icon directs children to stop and circle the best numeral they wrote.

To help them evaluate **9**, ask:
• Does your **9** have a round backward circle?
• Is your **9** straight up and down?

Repeat teaching steps 1 and 2 for numeral 10.

To help them evaluate **10**, ask:
• Is there a space between the **1** and **0** in your **10**?
• Does your **10** touch the headline and baseline?

Practice

1, 2, 3, 4, 5
Penguins jump and dive.

6, 7, 8, 9, 10
Then up they come again.

Trace and write.

1   2   3   4   5

6   7   8   9   10

110

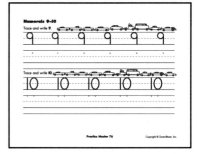

Apply

With the children, read the number verse at the top of student page 110. Help them recognize that there are ten penguins in the illustration on the page.

Review any numerals students are still having difficulty writing. Then ask them to trace and write the numerals in the space provided on the student page.

✓ **Stop and Check** To help children evaluate their numerals, ask:

• Do your numerals touch the headline and the baseline?
• Are your curved lines round?
• Are your vertical and horizontal lines straight?

Fun and Games

auditory   visual   kinesthetic

Using Manipulatives
Distribute to each child a sheet of paper with ten squares drawn on it. Provide precut colored construction paper squares (or other shapes), and have the children glue or paste a colored shape onto each of the ten squares. Encourage children to write a numeral on each square. (visual, kinesthetic)

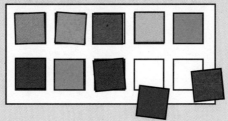

Walk the Line Make a large numeral **9** on the floor with some tape. Have the children walk on the line as if on a balance beam. (visual, kinesthetic)

Creative Movement Form a long line with the children. Ask the leader to call out a movement using a numeral from **1–10** (e.g., "Take three steps backward," "Jump ten times"). After the class follows the instructions, that leader goes to the back of the line. Continue until all the children have been leader. (visual, kinesthetic, auditory)

Write Numerals

Before Writing

Begin the lesson by having the children say a rhyme, such as this one:

1, 2, 3, 4, 5
I caught a fish alive.
6, 7, 8, 9, 10
I put it back again.

Prepare cards for the numerals **1–10** and show each numeral as you say its name in the rhyme. Then give a numeral card to a child. Have the children say the rhyme again with you, and ask the child with the numeral card to hold it up when the numeral's name is said. As the game catches on, add more cards until all ten numerals are represented.

In addition, you might create a center around Zaner-Bloser's interactive, write-on, wipe-off book *Now I Know My 1, 2, 3's.*

Write Numerals

How many? Write the numeral.

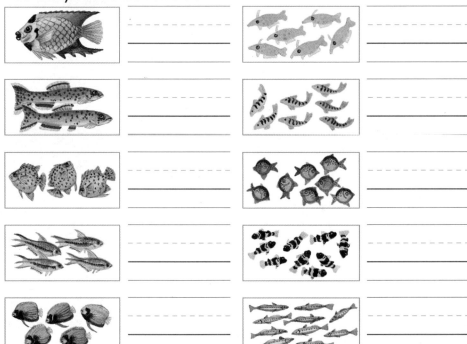

III

Present the Activity

Direct the children to look at the illustrations on student page 111. Point out that there are no models on the page. Tell children they can show they really know how to write their numerals when they can write them "by heart." Point out the writing space beside each illustration, and explain to the children that this is where they are to write the numeral that tells how many fish they count in each box.

Write and Evaluate

When they seem comfortable with the task, have the children complete the page by counting the fish in each box and writing the corresponding numeral in the space.

Ask children to look at the numerals they wrote and to circle the one they think is best. Encourage them to explain why they think that numeral might be better than the others.

Write Number Words

Write the numerals and number words.

 | one   2 two

 3 three   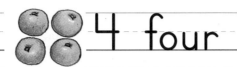 4 four

 5 five   6 six

112

Fun and Games

 auditory   visual   kinesthetic

Number Game Pair students for this activity. Tell one child to hold up any number of fingers while the second child says the numeral and then writes it on the chalkboard. Have the partners switch roles several times. (visual, auditory, kinesthetic)

Trace and Count Provide fun dough or clay and fill several bags with paper shapes, buttons, or other small items. Invite pairs of children to play a game: One child forms a numeral from **1–10** from the dough or clay, saying the strokes. The other child traces the numeral and counts out that number of objects from the bag. Then the children change roles. (kinesthetic, auditory, visual)

Number Line Road Make a number line to represent a road. Put the numerals **1–10** on small cars. Have the children place the cars in order on the number line road. (visual, kinesthetic)

Present the Activity

Have the children look at the illustrations, numerals, and words on student page 112. Read the directions with them, and help them recognize that each set of illustration, numeral, and word go together. Point out the writing space under each numeral and number word. Explain that this is where they are to write the numeral and number word for each illustration.

Note: Encourage children to continue writing numerals and number words for **7–10** on a separate sheet of paper, following your model. Alternately, use **Practice Masters 72–76**.

Write and Evaluate

When they seem comfortable with the task, have the children complete the page by writing the corresponding numeral and number word for each illustration.

Ask children to look at the numerals and number words they wrote and to circle a numeral or number word they think is best. Encourage them to explain why they think that choice might be better than the others.

Ideas for Fun and Functional Writing in the Kindergarten Classroom

As children progress in their ability to write uppercase and lowercase letters, they need plenty of opportunities to write for meaningful purposes. When children write something that others will read, they take pride in their handwriting and understand that it must be legible. Try these ideas for writing applications in your classroom.

- Help children use stickers to write rebus stories on chart paper to share with the class. Make a word bank of theme-related words for children to use in their stories.

- Invite each child to write and illustrate an ABC book. Collect the books in a class library and allow children to check out a classmate's book to read.

- Staple paper together to make an autograph book for each child. Allow time for children to write their names and draw pictures in each other's books.

- Ask children to help you prepare notes to send home to families. Have children address the notes or fill in key words they are learning to write.

- Provide index cards so that children can make labels for share items or class collections.

- Children like to make lists. Use chart paper to make individual, small group, or class lists of things such as favorite people, ice cream flavors, most prized possessions, names for pets, or ways to be helpful.

- Establish a working post office in your classroom. Provide a cardboard mailbox, stationery, old greeting cards, envelopes, and sticker "stamps" or use the Zaner-Bloser *Post Office Kit*. Allow time each day for the mail to be delivered.

- Have each child make an *Inch Book* that tells what is one inch long on the first page, what is two inches long on the second page, and so on, up to twelve inches. Provide rulers so that children can research an item for each page. Ask children to illustrate their books.

- Compose a class poem about springtime, a happy day, or special people. Provide a decorated page where children can write the poem in their best handwriting as a gift for someone they love.

- Help children create self-portraits and brief autobiographies to exchange with another kindergarten class in your building or area.

Write the words.

dog cat sun pig

113

Present the Activity

Direct the children to look at the illustration across the top of student page 113. Encourage discussion about what they see. Make sure they recognize the four characters represented: dog, cat, sun, pig.

Help children notice the characters across the middle of the page. Point out that each character has its word written beneath it. Encourage the children to name each character in turn and to notice the written word for it.

Write and Evaluate

Point out the writing space beneath each word on student page 113. Explain that this is where the children are to write the words. Encourage them to write their letters carefully and to follow the models for good writing.

Observe the children as they write. Check for correct sequence of strokes and that the strokes join to form each letter.

Alphabet Game Give each child a strip of paper with ruled lines. Have the children write their first names. Then have them add a word they like to write. Place all the names on a chart or pin them to the bulletin board. Help the children arrange the names in alphabetical order. As you name each letter of the alphabet, have the children find the names beginning with that letter. Arrange those names in order. When the names have been alphabetized, point to each name, say it, and have that child stand. Extend the activity by alphabetizing the words they wrote. (visual, auditory, kinesthetic)

Write Sentences

Write Sentences

Write the sentences.

One dog plays piano.

Three dogs sing.

114

Present the Activity

Point out the illustration at the top of student page 114. Ask the children to describe what they see.

Encourage volunteers to read aloud the sentences on the page. Ask if the information in the sentences agrees with what they see in the picture.

Write and Evaluate

Point out the writing space under each sentence. Explain that this is where they are to write the sentences. Direct the children to write the sentences in the space provided. Encourage them to write carefully so their sentences will be easy to read.

Show children how to leave a one-finger space between words.

Observe the children as they write. Check for correct sequence of strokes and that the strokes join to form each letter.

Coaching Hint

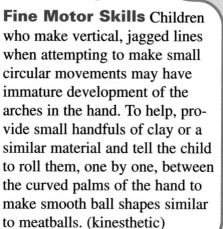

Fine Motor Skills Children who make vertical, jagged lines when attempting to make small circular movements may have immature development of the arches in the hand. To help, provide small handfuls of clay or a similar material and tell the child to roll them, one by one, between the curved palms of the hand to make smooth ball shapes similar to meatballs. (kinesthetic)

Write a Note

Write the note.

Dear Aunt Tess,

I miss you. Get well.

Sammy

115

Present the Activity

Direct children to look at the illustration and the writing on student page 115. Encourage them to describe what they see. Ask if any of the children have sent or received a note or a short letter.

Help the children identify the three main parts of the note on the student page. (*greeting, body, signature*) Ask volunteers to read each part of the note.

Write and Evaluate

Point out the writing space beneath each line of the note on student page 115. Explain that this is where the children are to write the note, using their best handwriting.

Show children how to leave a one-finger space between words and a two-finger space between sentences.

Observe the children as they write. Ask the children to tell which line of writing they think is their best, and encourage them to explain why they think so.

I Can Do It! Point out that the animals in the picture on student page 114 are doing special things. Have the children think of special things they can do. Ask them to draw pictures of themselves doing these things. Under each picture, help them write a caption telling what the activity is. (auditory, kinesthetic)

Write an Invitation

Write an Invitation

Write the invitation.

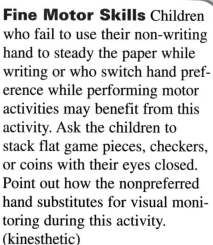

Come to our party.

It will be on Friday.

We will have fun.

116

Present the Activity

Point out the illustration at the top of student page 116. Encourage discussion about what the children see. Help them recognize that the children in the picture are at a party.

Explain that the sentences on the page are an invitation. Have volunteers read each sentence.

Write and Evaluate

Read the directions for writing on student page 116. When you are sure children know what to do, have them write the invitation.

Observe the children as they write. Tell the children to look over their sentences and check that each one begins with an uppercase letter and ends with an end-of-sentence punctuation mark.

Encourage children to point out the sentence they think is written best and to explain why they think so.

Coaching Hint

Fine Motor Skills Children who fail to use their non-writing hand to steady the paper while writing or who switch hand preference while performing motor activities may benefit from this activity. Ask the children to stack flat game pieces, checkers, or coins with their eyes closed. Point out how the nonpreferred hand substitutes for visual monitoring during this activity. (kinesthetic)

Write a Weather Report

| warm |
| cold |
| sunny |
| rainy |

Choose words to complete the sentences. Write the sentences.

Today is _____.

It is _____ outside.

117

Present the Activity

Direct the children to look at the illustrations at the top of student page 117. Encourage them to describe what they see. Point out the word bank between the two illustrations. Ask volunteers to tell about the information it contains.

Have other volunteers read the words on the page. Make sure children recognize that spaces have been left open for them to write their own weather words. Ask the children to identify words from the word bank to describe the current weather outside.

Write and Evaluate

When you are sure the children understand what they are to do, have them write the weather report on student page 117, filling in the appropriate words for the weather conditions.

Have the children choose several words they wrote on the page and evaluate their writing by comparing the size and shape of their letters with the models. Help the children recognize why one word is better than another.

It's a Party! Encourage the children to think of a party they would like to have. Help them think of information they need to include on the invitations they would give to their friends, such as the date and time of the party and where the party will be. Provide paper and art materials and have the children write and decorate their invitations. (auditory, visual, kinesthetic)

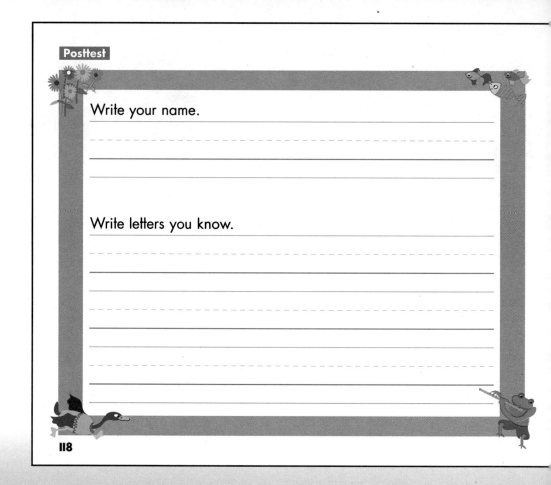

Write your name.

Write letters you know.

118

Present the Activity

Explain to the children that at the beginning of the year, on student page 9, they drew a picture and wrote letters they knew. Have them turn to page 9 to review their work on that page.

Direct the children's attention to student pages 118 and 119. Point out the directions and spaces for response. Then read the directions with the children, making sure they understand the task.

Before the children write, encourage a lively sharing of ideas about the different subjects they might choose to draw and write about.

Write and Draw

Have the children write their name and then write their best letters in the spaces provided on student page 118. Encourage them to write carefully so their names and letters will be easy to read.

Provide a variety of drawing materials, and have the children draw a picture in the space provided on student page 119. Then ask them to write about their picture. Accept the use of invented spellings.

Evaluate

Guide the children in evaluating their writing. Then ask if they can read their writing easily. Encourage them to explain why or why not.

When they have finished the pages, you might want to have them compare their work in the posttest with what they did in the pretest on student page 9. Invite them to share their thoughts about what they have accomplished in handwriting.

Some children may wish to share their pictures and stories with their classmates.

Draw a picture.
Write words about your picture.

119

Sand Writing Fill a baking pan or cookie sheet with sand or other fine-grain material. Encourage the children to make lines, circles, and letters in the sand. Then have individual children look at a letter you have written on an index card and write that letter in the sand, using correct formation and sequencing of the strokes. (kinesthetic, visual)

Coaching Hints
Hands-On Handwriting

For children who are still having difficulty forming letters, write a letter on guidelines on poster board or cardboard and laminate it. Children can use the letterforms as a base for making the letters with clay. Have the children trace their completed letters and say the stroke descriptions. (kinesthetic, auditory, visual)

Make an audiotape of letter names and stroke descriptions and provide a tape player. Have children who still need practice with individual letters listen to the tape and write the letters described. (auditory, kinesthetic)

Prepare tactile letters or sandpaper letters, or use Zaner-Bloser's *Touch and Trace Letter Cards*. Have the children close their eyes, touch a letter, and identify it by its size and shape. You may need to guide a child's direction in exploring letter shape. (kinesthetic)

Use chalk to write any tricky letters in a large size on the playground pavement. Invite children to walk or hop along the letter in the correct sequence to reinforce good letter formation. (kinesthetic)

Making sandpaper letters and having children trace them as you say the stroke descriptions is helpful to children who have problems with small-muscle coordination and difficulty in writing the letters. (auditory, kinesthetic)

Fun and Games

auditory   visual   kinesthetic

Letter Puzzles Have children work in pairs to use their Basic Strokes pieces to assemble specific letters, such as the letter **E**. Discuss the formation of the letter, using the vertical stroke first, then adding the top, bottom, and shorter middle horizontal strokes. Have one child give directions while the other assembles the letter. Then have the children reverse roles. (auditory, visual, kinesthetic)

Index

120

Teacher Notes

Teacher Notes

Teacher Notes

Teacher Notes